Evaluating Services for Survivors of Domestic Violence and Sexual Assault

Sage Series on Violence Against Women

Series Editors

Claire M. Renzetti
St. Joseph's University

Jeffrey L. Edleson
University of Minnesota

Stephanie Riger • Larry Bennett
Sharon M. Wasco • Paul A. Schewe
Lisa Frohmann • Jennifer M. Camacho
Rebecca Campbell
University of Illinois at Chicago

Evaluating Services for Survivors of Domestic Violence and Sexual Assault

Sage Series on Violence Against Women

SAGE Publications
International Educational and Professional Publisher
Thousand Oaks ▪ London ▪ New Delhi

For information:

Sage Publications, Inc.
2455 Teller Road
Thousand Oaks, California 91320
E-mail: order@sagepub.com

Sage Publications Ltd.
6 Bonhill Street
London EC2A 4PU
United Kingdom

Sage Publications India Pvt. Ltd.
M-32 Market
Greater Kailash I
New Delhi 110 048 India

Printed in the United States of America

Library of Congress Cataloging-in-Publication Data

Evaluating services for survivors of domestic violence and sexual assault / by Stephanie Riger . . . [et al].
    p. cm. -- (Sage series on violence against women)
Includes bibliographical references and index.
  ISBN 0-7619-2352-7 (c) -- ISBN 0-7619-2353-5 (p)
  1. Abused women--Services for--United States--Evaluation.
  2. Sexual abuse victims--Services for--United States--Evaluation. I. Riger, Stephanie. II. Series.
  HV6626.2 .E93 2002
  362.82´92´0973—dc21

                                                   2002001787

This book is printed on acid-free paper.

02 03 04 05 10 9 8 7 6 5 4 3 2 1

Acquisitions Editor:	Margaret Seawell
Editorial Assistant:	Alicia Carter
Production Editors:	Claudia A. Hoffman and Olivia Weber
Copy Editor:	Amy Kasilsky
Typesetter:	Siva Math Setters, Chennai, India
Indexer:	Teri Greenberg
Cover Designer:	Sandra Ng

Contents

Foreword

Thirty years into the effort to end violence against women, very significant social, legislative, and political advances that improve justice and increase safety for those who experience domestic violence and sexual assault can be celebrated. In large part, these changes can be attributed to the grassroots, feminist movement that privileged the experience and leadership of those women who survived abuse. Subsequently, efforts designed to respond to the problems of battering and rape have assumed a prominent place on the national policy agenda, resulting in the passing of federal legislation that provides funding for services, the establishment of research and academic research centers, and the introduction of public initiatives by the United States Department of Health and Human Services, Centers for Disease Control, Department of Justice, Housing and Urban Development, Department of Defense, and other agencies in response to their recognition of the serious health and social consequences of violence against women.

A national, multilingual hotline has been established and receives calls from victims in need of emergency assistance, concerned family members, and community-based advocates. Local programs are flooded with similar calls. Most important, grassroots activism has led to a lively network of service providers (some who have celebrated more than 30 years of advocacy and activism) who continue to push for social change and shifts in public consciousness around violence against women and broader issues of gender inequality.

With these important advances has come the challenge to evaluate the broad-based mobilization in general terms and to assess the effectiveness of direct service delivery programs in particular. Many long-term advocates and activists—especially those who continue to respond to women in crisis—have raised the following questions. Has our work for the past 30 years made a difference? Do treatment programs for abusers work? Do crisis intervention programs have a long-term impact? Are families safer and stronger, and are communities more nurturing and attentive to the needs of women and girls? Are more women and children free from the terror that accompanies constant physical, emotional, sexual, and economic abuse because of our work? Have all women benefited equally, regardless of race and ethnicity, sexual orientation, or social status? Have there been unintended negative consequences from our work and what antiviolence strategies will take us into the future? These are the questions that frame this book. What appears at first glance to be a volume about evaluating services is actually much, much more; it is one with tremendous appeal and broad significance.

In addition to reviewing the basic concepts related to evaluation, *Evaluating Services for Survivors of Domestic Violence and Sexual Assault* is a chronicle of the antiviolence movement and the development of services. By focusing in one volume on both domestic violence and sexual assault, it makes an important conceptual intervention by challenging readers to be more comprehensive when thinking about this work. In a similar way, the authors are both researchers and practitioners who represent various disciplines. The text, therefore, reflects a multidisciplinary, multimethod approach to evaluation. It does so in a way that demystifies research, models collaboration, and promotes dialogue between the various constituencies who work to end violence against women. Although it clearly and convincingly stresses the importance of evaluation, it does so in a way that emphasizes the need for safety and confidentiality; readers will walk away from the text understanding how important it is to listen to women's voices, to build individual and organizational trust, to respect differences, and to link evaluation to intervention reform and policy changes. The honest consideration of agencies' constraints, the willingness to name contradictory roles, and the look to the future of evaluation as a key aspect of this work are tremendously important and refreshing. I expect that *Evaluating Services for Survivors of Domestic Violence and Sexual Assault* will assume a key place in the scholarship on evaluation, and will make a tremendous contribution to grassroots service providers working to end violence against women.

Beth Richie, Ph.D.
University of Illinois at Chicago

For years on end, I talked about the unfailing commitment of domestic violence programs to saving lives, about the value of these services to women and children across the state. And I talked about the incredible number of clients served, the number of hotline calls, shelter nights, and so on. But within the context of evidence-based programming, the new era for all of us, those statements didn't hold water. Now when I'm asked to prove it, or when I look for new funding (everyday), I have something besides gut feelings to rely upon. And so do our providers. What gratifies me most is observing them using the results of the evaluation and the performance measures in other venues, with other funders and potential funders. After all the blood and sweat, we all got to be winners.

Carol Brigman
Chief, Bureau of Domestic Violence
Prevention and Intervention
Illinois Department of Human Services

Introduction

In May 1998, the Illinois Department of Human Services (DHS) decided to evaluate its state-funded sexual assault and domestic violence programs. Several concerns prompted this decision. DHS was investing a considerable portion of its resources in domestic violence and sexual assault services, yet little was known about the overall impact of those services. Were clients obtaining the services they needed? Were those services helping women? Was taxpayers' money being spent wisely?

The authors of this book were selected to conduct this evaluation in part because we all have had experience conducting research on violence against women and evaluation research, as well as histories of collaborating with advocates and service providers. Our work on this project over a three-year period taught us much about evaluating services for victimized women. We learned the extreme care with which research must be designed to ensure that research methods do not put women in danger or interfere with their recovery. Safety, confidentiality, and well-being of clients must supersede evaluation considerations. We attempted, whenever possible, to develop the evaluation collaboratively with practitioners, and we learned about the value (and the challenges) of such collaborations.

Although members of our group share a commitment to ending violence against women, we differ in many ways. Some of us prefer quantitative research methods whereas others prefer qualitative ones. We come from different disciplinary backgrounds: psychology, criminal justice, and social work. Some of us have a history of working against sexual assault; others have had more experience in working against domestic violence. We share a strong commitment to using research skills to prevent and reduce violence and to help the survivors of abuse. Over the years that we have worked on this project, we have had many stimulating discussions about the nature and process of evaluation. We hope to pass on through this book not only our expertise in evaluation but also the deeper issues that underlie many decisions in the course of an evaluation.

Perhaps the most important lesson that we learned is that evaluation always occurs in context. Resources available within an agency may affect the scope of an evaluation because data collection puts demands for time and effort on an already burdened staff. Within the violence against women movement, the press for evaluation may have consequences for future interventions. Funders' requirement that services be evaluated may exert a push for easily measurable goals and individual services because those may require less effort to show success compared to more elusive goals such as prevention. Also, evaluation may conflict with providers' service philosophy. Many practitioners consider themselves to be client centered, letting clients determine the direction of interactions. They may see asking evaluation questions as putting the needs of the agency ahead of those of the client (albeit temporarily). Evaluation of programs offering services to abused women thus may raise issues not seen in other contexts.

Our purpose here is twofold. First, we discuss the special considerations that evaluators must take into account when researching domestic violence and sexual assault. At the same time, we aim to persuade service providers of the value of evaluation. Second, we illustrate both how to do an evaluation of services for victims of interpersonal violence and the difficult choices that must be made in that process. We believe that this will be helpful not only to providers of services but also to evaluators who must operate within similar constraints. Thus, although our experience is based on our research in Illinois, the issues raised in this book are widely applicable.

In sum, this book is trying to accomplish what some say is impossible—meeting the needs of two audiences: practitioners and evaluators (and possibly even a third, funders). Material useful to all of these audiences is in every chapter of this book. Evaluators may be tempted to skip the chapters on "why evaluate" or "how to evaluate," thinking that they already have that expertise. But the blending into these chapters of issues that are unique to domestic violence and sexual assault makes them essential reading for anyone who wants to work in this area. Alternatively, practitioners may not feel the need to read the chapter on the movements against violence against women. Yet we believe that serious attention must be paid to the potential impact of evaluation on the direction of those movements.

The first part of the book discusses the social and political context of evaluation because of our belief that it is crucial to the success of an evaluation. We examine the evolution of the domestic violence and sexual assault movements over the last 30 years and the emergence of services for abused women. The sexual assault and domestic violence movements have somewhat different (though overlapping) histories and concerns; therefore, we consider them separately in Chapter 1. We then discuss in Chapter 2 issues that arise in the collaboration between practitioners and researchers when an evaluation is conducted jointly. These two chapters draw on previous research as well as our experience in Illinois. Part II moves to practical concerns in conducting an evaluation. Chapters 3 and 4 focus on "why evaluate" and "basic concepts in evaluation." Chapter 5 considers ways to use the results to improve agencies and attract clients and funding. Part III considers the lessons learned from our experience in Illinois that are generally applicable to evaluating domestic violence and sexual assault services. Chapter 6 discusses the problems and possibilities of the measures that we developed for use in Illinois, and we present those measures in Appendices A and B. More information, evaluation resources, and English and Spanish versions of the evaluation measures as well as statistical analyses of the measures, and consent forms, are available on our web site: www.uic.edu/depts/psch/idhs.

We have gained valuable input from other evaluators working on similar projects, including *Evaluating Domestic Violence Programs*, an evaluation manual for domestic violence service providers that emerged from the Domestic Abuse Project in Minnesota (Edleson & Frick, 1997), which differed from our work most significantly in that it did not include sexual assault services. We also drew from the Sexual Assault and Rape Prevention Evaluation Project in Michigan (Campbell, Davidson, et al., 1998; Campbell, Davidson, et al., 1999), an empowerment evaluation project providing consultation, evaluation training, and technical assistance to sexual assault programs. This project differed from ours in that it worked with sexual assault programs but did not include domestic violence programs. Additionally, we examined outcome measures for domestic violence services developed for the Pennsylvania Coalition Against Domestic Violence (Sullivan, 1998). The Urban Institute was contracted by the National Institute of Justice to conduct an evaluation of the STOP grants funded by the 1994 Violence Against Women Act. To date, this work has included process evaluations of all STOP grantees in all 50 states. Although this work was useful to us, our task was to develop outcome, not process evaluation, measures. Finally, our work focused only on services to survivors of sexual assault and domestic violence, not prevention, interventions with batterers, or community efforts. For a guide to evaluating the latter, see Garske et al. (2000).

We are grateful to the staff, volunteers, and clients of the 87 sexual assault and domestic violence agencies in Illinois that participated in the evaluation; to James Nelson, JoAnne Durkee, Carol Brigman, and Susan Catania at the Illinois Department of Human Services for their unflagging support; to the Illinios Coalition Against Sexual Assault and their agencies and to Illinois domestic violence agencies for their many suggestions and cooperation; and to April Howard and Mark Thomas for invaluable research assistance. We thank Linda Hauser of Willamette University in Oregon for generously sharing her literature review of more than 100 studies evaluating domestic violence and sexual assault programs. We are especially grateful to the many abused women whose patience and cooperation made this evaluation project possible. In their honor, we are contributing all royalties that accrue from this book to a fund to support graduate student research at the University of Illinois at Chicago on violence against women.

PART I:
The Political and Social Context of Evaluation

1

The Evolution of the Violence Against Women Social Movement and Services for Victims

To place our evaluation of sexual assault and domestic violence services in context, this chapter provides a brief overview of the historical development of the violence against women social movements. In both the antirape movement and the battered women's movement, two key activities dominated the early efforts of community activists. First, volunteers established rape crisis centers (RCCs) and domestic violence shelters to provide crisis services for victimized women. Starting as grassroots efforts, these agencies have grown in number and complexity. Here we review the challenges and successes in creating these centers and shelters. Second, agency staff and other advocates have pushed for reform of federal and state legal statutes that pertain to violence against women. We will highlight pivotal legislative reforms and briefly review the effectiveness of those changes in addressing the needs of victimized women. Following this historical introduction, we will focus on the primary services offered by today's rape crisis centers and domestic violence shelters. Finally, we conclude this chapter with an overview of how the violence against women social movements have responded to the increased demand for program evaluation and discuss some of the challenges in evaluating community services for rape survivors and battered women.

THE HISTORY OF THE VIOLENCE
AGAINST WOMEN MOVEMENTS

In the United States, the violence against women social movements emerged from the women's movement of the late 1960s and early 1970s. Although the specific historical development of the antirape movement and battered women's movement varied, they shared an underlying connection with the feminist movement more generally. Two themes in the women's movement—women's rights feminism and women's liberation feminism—shaped the philosophies and social change activities of the developing antirape and battered women's movement. Women's rights feminism emphasized the inequality between men and women as a fundamental concern and advocated for civil and political equality within existing social systems. The women's liberation branch of the movement focused on women's oppression and worked for women's self-determination. This perspective saw men's power as a dynamic force that created and maintained itself through interaction and reproduced itself through policy, law, and other institutional structures. Women's liberation feminists sought equality through a total restructuring of society.

Both of these approaches to feminist social change were instrumental in helping the early violence against women activists raise awareness that rape and battering were social problems needing public attention. Specifically, activists in the early violence against women social movements focused on two key efforts: establishing rape crisis hotlines, centers, and shelters for victims of violence and advocating for legal reform in crimes against women. Activists focused on these areas because of society's attitudes toward violence against women, the lack of services for women who needed to leave abusive situations, inadequate laws, and medical and legal procedures that made women feel revictimized by the systems they turned to for help.

Historical Development of the Antirape Movement

The first U.S. RCCs were formed in the 1970s to provide services to victims in crisis, educate communities about violence against women, and mobilize efforts for social change. Truly a grassroots effort, many of the first RCCs were run out of women's own homes with donated materials (e.g., telephones, furniture, printing for fliers) (O'Sullivan, 1978; Pride, 1981). The staff of these early centers were often community volunteers who did not have counseling or professional service backgrounds. Women joined these groups because they were committed to helping victims and to changing society (Gornick, Burt, & Pittman, 1985; Matthews, 1994; Riger, 1984).

In contrast to traditional social service agencies, many of these fledging centers were run as feminist collectives in which members of the organization shared power and decision making (see Koss & Harvey, 1991). Early RCCs tried developing less hierarchical organizational practices; as a result, more traditional social service agency structures, such as appointing an executive director or forming a board of directors, were not commonly used (Koss & Harvey, 1991). Similarly, many of these organizations were freestanding agencies, completely autonomous and not affiliated with or dependent on a parent organization (e.g., a YWCA, hospital, mental health agency). In fact, many centers were suspicious of the underlying motives and support offered by mainstream organizations (Byington, Martin, DiNitto, & Maxwell, 1991; Martin, DiNitto, Byington, & Maxwell, 1992; Matthews, 1994; Schechter, 1982). Even without the support of established social service agencies and government funding, RCCs continued to grow in numbers throughout the United States.

As time passed, many of the original leaders of the antirape movement grew tired from years of struggle for the cause (Gornick et al., 1985; Matthews, 1994). As some left, many of the new women who became involved valued a more conventional and apolitical approach. With this new diversity, varied visions emerged for the structure and function of RCCs (Gornick et al., 1985; Koss & Harvey, 1991; O'Sullivan, 1978). The shift from radical social change agencies to social service organizations happened in varying degrees over many years. By the mid-1970s, many centers began applying for and receiving Law Enforcement Assistance Administration (LEAA) and United Way funding (Gornick et al., 1985; Matthews, 1994; O'Sullivan, 1978; Pride, 1981). Government funding to RCCs brought three related changes. First, many centers moved from collectives to hierarchical organizational structures, designating executive directors, program coordinators, and boards of directors with formal decision-making power over members, programs, and policies (Collins & Whalen, 1989; O'Sullivan, 1978; Pride, 1981). Second, with the move from collectives to traditional structures came a shift in staffing. Government and other funding sources stressed the importance of professionally certified personnel. It was no longer enough for staff to be former rape victims committed to empowering women; they now had to be trained and certified as professionals or paraprofessionals (Collins & Whalen, 1989). Third, with external funding came the need for affiliation with an organization that could provide fiscal accountability (Byington et al., 1991). Many formerly freestanding centers became affiliated with or were absorbed by agencies such as YWCAs, community mental health centers, hospitals, and district attorney's offices (Gornick et al., 1985; Matthews, 1994; Pride, 1981; Schechter, 1982).

Although the antirape movement experienced a general shift toward professionalization, individual centers varied in how much they changed their structures and functions. For instance, not all centers changed to hierarchical structures with hired professionals. In one of the first studies on this professionalization shift, O'Sullivan (1978) surveyed 90 completely autonomous RCCs that had been founded prior to 1976. Even though these centers had started receiving substantial government fiscal support, only 43% had a board of directors. Most centers favored steering committees over a board of directors as they saw this format as less hierarchical and more consistent with feminist collective ideology.

In the 1980s, Gornick et al. (1985) surveyed a sample of 50 nationally representative rape crisis centers (see also Harvey, 1985). Since O'Sullivan's research, more variation had emerged in organizational structures, staff composition, and funding sources. Gornick et al. (1985) identified four types of rape crisis centers: (a) programs resembling the original feminist collectives of the 1970s; (b) programs more mainstream and traditional in structure (i.e., bureaucratic); (c) programs embedded in a social service or mental health agency; and (d) programs based in hospital emergency rooms. Furthermore, Gornick et al.'s results revealed that independent centers were more politically active than affiliated centers, and collectively run centers were more service oriented than bureaucratic centers (see also Bordt, 1997). Matthews (1994) found similar findings in her historical study of six rape crisis centers in Los Angeles. Matthews argued that rape crisis work had been influenced by a conservative service delivery approach because of the ongoing struggle between the antirape movement and the state. Centers that started out with different styles and perspectives soon became similar as RCCs developed consistent procedures and bureaucratic structures in response to government funding requirements (see DiMaggio & Powell, 1991).

In the 1990s, Campbell, Baker, and Mazurek (1998) continued to find evidence of this shift toward homogenized professionalization. In a study of 168 rape crisis centers throughout the country, they found a cohort effect that differentiated centers formed in the peak of the antirape movement (1978 or earlier) from those founded in 1979 or later, a more conservative era in U.S. politics. The older centers had larger budgets and more staff but were more likely to be freestanding collectives. Their internal communication style was more likely to stress participatory decision making as all members of the organization, from the board of directors to the volunteers and clients, were involved. Older centers were also more likely than newer centers to participate in social change activities, such as public demonstrations against violence against women and rape prevention programming. The newer centers had comparatively smaller budgets and staffing levels and were more likely to be hierarchical organizations affiliated with larger social service agencies. Internal decisions in these agencies were made without the participation of the less powerful members of the organization (e.g., volunteers and clients). These newer centers were less likely to be engaged in public demonstrations or prevention work but were more likely than the older centers to be involved in lobbying elected politicians. The top-down approach of political lobbying may be more consistent with these newer organizations' philosophies than the grassroots tactics favored by older centers. These results suggest that some RCCs have altered their structures and functions since the beginnings of the antirape movement but that these changes may have been necessary to survive the different political climates of the 1980s and 1990s. The staff of many of these centers may have felt that deradicalizing was key to long-term organizational sustainability in an era of increasingly conservative state politics (see Spalter-Roth & Schreiber, 1995).

In addition to establishing rape crisis centers, a second major effort in the early antirape movement was to advocate for legal reform in federal and state rape statutes. Activists and scholars hoped that reform of legal statutes, the criminal justice system, and collateral institutions would facilitate the reporting of sexual assaults, encourage prosecution, and increase convictions. These reforms were intended to challenge the cultural and political ideology that tolerated and supported violence against women. The typical reforms in statutory rape law included a number of changes. In many states, rape was redefined from a single offense to a gradation of offenses with commensurate penalties. The requirement that a victim's testimony be corroborated by another witness was eliminated. The consent standard was changed to modify or eliminate the requirement that women physically resist their perpetrators. Rape shield laws that restricted the introduction of evidence about a woman's past sexual history into trial testimony were enacted (Spohn & Horney, 1992). By removing the bases for discrediting or blaming women when they reported rape, these legal reforms aimed to make sexual assault more prosecutable and to treat women like victims of other kinds of crime.

Legislative reform has improved women's experiences in the legal system (Largen, 1988; Marsh, Geist, & Kaplan, 1982; Spohn & Horney, 1992). Nevertheless, studies that have examined the rates of reporting, prosecution, and conviction before and after rape law reform suggest mixed results of reform. For example, in Washington State, Loh (1981) found an increase in the conviction rate for rape and a decrease in other offenses. He suggests this is the result of a change in labeling of conviction, as men are now being convicted of rape instead of other offenses. On the whole, no change in charging decisions or in the overall conviction of rape cases took place. Loh also reported that criminal justice officials were using the same criteria for making charging decisions before and after the reform (i.e., force, victim–offender relationship, corroborative evidence, victim's credibility, and race). Marsh et al. (1982) found that although the number of rapes reported to the police had not changed, the rate of the convictions and the number of arrests had increased. The law had much less effect on the factors prosecutors considered when making filing decisions, specifically regarding a victim's sexual history. This information still found its way into the courtroom. Polk (1985) found that, in California, police clearance rates for rape did not change. Complaint filings increased slightly but the probability of conviction, once a case reached court, was unchanged. Yet, if a rapist was convicted, harsher sentences were handed down. This trend may be part of a general shift toward harsher penalties for all serious felonies. Spohn and Horney (1992) examined six cities in the United States (Chicago, Houston, Washington D.C., Philadelphia, Atlanta, and Detroit). Excluding Detroit, rape reform did not increase rape reporting, prosecutions, convictions, or incarcerations. In Detroit, reforms had limited effect. The number of rape reports, and the maximum sentence for those incarcerated, increased whereas conviction or incarceration rates saw no change.

Explanations for limited instrumental effects of legal rape reform vary. Berger, Searles, and Neuman (1988) suggest that the more radical elements of reform initially envisioned by feminists were diluted to enable them to work in coalitions with law enforcement officials to push for change. This process continued as the reforms went through the legislature. Spohn and Horney (1992) argue that reform-oriented changes were already underway through case decisions before final reform was instituted.

These explanations focus on the constraints in the law-making process, suggesting that if the laws were better the results would be better. Other researchers have focused on what practitioners do with the law and argue that simply rewriting law is not enough. Spohn and

Horney (1992) suggest that statutory reforms do not affect the courtroom work group and the informal norms of case processing. Similarly, Frohmann (1991, 1996) found that concerns of prosecutors, such as their assessments of the convictability of cases and their expectations about jurors' beliefs, had a chilling effect on the prosecution of sexual assault cases despite rape law reform. Organizational structures and practical work concerns shape decision-making practices.

Matoesian (1995) argues that reforms do not address the deep structures and symbolic constructions through which people make sense of a rape. He argues that power, domination, and patriarchy are constructed and maintained in and through courtroom talk and that these linguistic structures are essential to understanding the power relations between victim and assailant, men and women, and dominant and subordinate groups. The failure of legal reform to address these cultural constructs limits its ability to create change. What Spohn and Horney, Matoesian, and Frohmann suggest is a disjuncture between rules (i.e., legal statutes) and practice. Change in legal statutes does not necessarily translate into a change in everyday decision making and the ways legal agents perceive their responsibilities. Each of these researchers points to the need to examine the organizational subculture to understand this disjuncture.

Martin and Powell (1994) take up this call. One of the goals of rape reform is to make the system more victim sensitive (attentive to victims' needs and well-being). Martin and Powell examine the work of legal and medical professionals to assess whether this goal has been met. They found that, in spite of agents' good intentions, they were not sensitive to victims' needs. Martin and Powell attribute this to the organizational culture of the legal and medical agencies that orient staff toward practical work concerns such as winning cases or political concerns like public opinion. They argue that organizational concerns shape legal practitioners' decision making more than statutory reform. They suggest that in order to effect deep change, we need a nationwide discourse on the "politics of rape victims' needs" (Martin & Powell, 1994) to address gender inequality underlying violence against women and the legal system's response to victims.

In spite of the legal changes and new medical and legal protocols, the limited change in organizational culture means that rape crisis center services are as important as ever. The information and support provided by rape crisis hotlines and medical and legal advocates provides a safe, nonjudgmental, and informative way for women, their families, and significant others to talk with people about their experiences and concerns. In addition, agencies also provide counseling and support groups for women and provide prevention education in schools, hospitals, criminal justice agencies, and the broader community.

Historical Development of the Battered Women's Movement

The U.S. battered women's social movement was influenced by the American antirape movement as well as by international efforts to create domestic violence shelters. In England, the Chiswick Women's Aid group emerged as a national, and ultimately international, model for domestic violence services. The Chiswick group, which came together initially to protest the elimination of free school milk, began sharing their stories of violence. Other women in the group opened their homes to provide refuge for battered women and, through continued community organization, the Chiswick Women's Aid group raised awareness about the problem of woman battering and secured resources for public refuge houses. Erin Pizzey emerged as a powerful leader of this group and her book, *Scream Quietly or the Neighbours Will Hear* (1974), became a resource for women's groups in Great Britain and the United States.

This English model was critical to the battered women's movement in the United States. Schechter (1982) noted that activists in the United States were frustrated that, for battered women and children, there seemed to be "no place to go." Existing social service networks in America did not have the interest or resources to address the problem of domestic violence. Many cities throughout the country had general emergency shelters, homeless shelters, or both, but the staff at these shelters had little training or preparation for working with battered women and their children. Thus, the initial efforts of the movement focused almost exclusively on providing refuge and creating shelters specifically for battered women (Dobash & Dobash, 1979, 1992; Martin, 1976; Pagelow, 1981; Schechter, 1982). This task was difficult not only because of the challenges of raising funds and finding a safe place to house women, but also due to the staggering lack of community support for the issue. Schechter (1982) described how numerous local organizing groups experienced difficulties with realtors who would not help activists find houses that could be converted to shelters and, even when a community could find a shelter home, it was not uncommon to run into further difficulty with local zoning boards. Domestic violence was seen as a private issue, a family matter that should be handled within the privacy of marriage without community intervention. This public attitude was not as problematic for the early antirape movement, which focused quite heavily on stranger rape and thereby did not challenge the norms regarding violence between intimate partners. The early battered women's movement had no choice but to address this issue directly, making intimate partner violence a public social issue.

With respect to accepting government funding, the early battered women's programs had to wrestle with different concerns than did many of the early rape crisis centers. It was, and continues to be, quite costly to open and maintain a shelter for women and children. The costs of running a safe house are considerably higher than a hotline, which at the time was the primary service of rape crisis centers. Domestic violence service providers needed space (such as a large house) and other material goods like food, linens, and household supplies. The reliance on public funding also meant that many of the early domestic violence shelters had quasi-social service agency structures. Similar to the early rape crisis centers, many shelters tried to operate with less hierarchical structures but accountability for fiscal matters required separation of roles and responsibilities. Early funding for domestic violence shelters came from local groups, such as YMCA/YWCAs and the United Way, which often required more formal organizational structures of the agencies they supported. These grants were not typically large enough to maintain a shelter's budget, so many costs were covered by private donations secured through extensive fund-raising (Dobash & Dobash, 1979, 1992; Schechter, 1982). With successful advocacy, county and state funds became available in the late 1970s and early 1980s. Such support provided resources for shelter as well as for staff to work on legal and institutional advocacy. However, in the mid- to late-1980s, many shelters faced dramatic cuts in their hard-earned budgets. This more conservative era in American politics brought attacks against feminism and the "welfare state." Shelter staff and volunteers were forced to redirect much of their attention to fund-raising and fighting these budget cuts.

In addition to establishing domestic violence shelters, early efforts in the battered women's movement focused on legal reform. Similar to the antirape movement, the reasons for this focus were attorneys' and other court personnel's dismissal of women's requests for assistance, the legal void when it came to considering battering as a crime, and societal perceptions of battering as a private matter. Like the civil rights movement, the violence against women movement believed that social change could be leveraged through legal change. Thus a key effort by the battered women's movement was instituting mandatory or proarrest policies that would require police officers to arrest batterers when domestic assault had occurred. Two major lawsuits in 1976 and 1984 won damages against police departments for failing to protect battered women. Feminist advocates confronted police departments with charges of ineffective responses to battered women and argued for training and laws requiring arrest. Research by Sherman and Berk (1984) assisted in launching this policy by arguing that arrest was a significantly more effective deterrent of future arrest than separation or mediation. However, these findings have been widely critiqued (see Binder & Meeker, 1988; Bowman, 1992; Frisch, 1992; Miller, 1989; Zorza, 1992) and evaluations of mandatory arrest polices have produced inconclusive findings. Many researchers argue that deterrent effects of arrest are minimal (Buzawa & Buzawa, 1990, 1993; Dunford, 1992; Dunford, Huizinga, & Elliot, 1990; Gelles, 1993; Hilton, 1994; Hirschel & Hutchison, 1992; Sherman, Schmidt, & Rogan, 1992). Regardless of the long-term deterrent effects, for many women, the short-term gain is sufficient to justify the policy.

However, mandatory arrest policies may have a number of unintended consequences. Often, police arrest both the battered woman and her batterer to avoid deciding who is responsible (Bourg & Stock, 1994; Buzawa & Buzawa, 1990; Ferraro, 1989a, 1989b). Moreover, police respond differentially to battering calls depending on the race, ethnicity, and class of the woman. They are less likely to respond to calls from black women and low-income minority women but when they do respond, police are more likely to arrest men of color than white men. For low-income women, arrest of the batterer may mean a loss of income and housing, leading to homelessness (Miller, 1993; Rasche, 1988; Stanko, 1989). Immigrant women fear that if they call the police, the Immigration and Naturalization Services will be notified, which could lead to deportation for them or their spouses, loss of dependant immigrant or residential status, or loss of access to their children (Abraham, 2000; Erez, 2000; Ferraro, 1989a, 1989b; Narayan, 1995).

Other legal reforms besides mandatory arrest have been enacted and evaluated. Temporary restraining orders (TROs), a civil law procedure, and orders of protection, a criminal law procedure by which abused women can restrict batterers' contact with them, have become widely available. Studies on the effectiveness of temporary restraining orders and orders of protection have also produced mixed results. Researchers found temporary restraining orders to be successful with men in early stages of battering and those without alcohol or drug problems (Chaudhuri & Daly, 1992; Klein, 1996). Others have found that men who had prior convictions, were unemployed or partially employed, or abused drugs or alcohol were more likely to batter women again (Chaudhuri & Daly, 1992; Harre & Smith, 1996; Keiltitz, Davis, Efkeman, Flango, & Hannaford, 1998). Also, women, particularly women of color and poor women, have trouble getting their protective orders enforced (Finn & Colson, 1990; Harre & Smith, 1996; Hart, 1996; Kinports & Fischer, 1993). On a positive note, TROs help empower women to end their abusive relationships if they are not economically and emotionally dependent on men (Chaudhuri & Daly, 1992; Fischer & Rose, 1995; Keiltitz et al., 1998).

These legal tools, although helpful for some women, have not ended battering. Women's need for safe refuge has not been eliminated and the current number of beds available for women and their children in shelters is inadequate. Thus a central activity of the battered women's movement continues to be running shelters. Shelters also provide needed services, such as counseling, housing and employment assistance, legal advocacy, and child care while women move toward independence. These services are also available to women who are not living in a shelter. Legal changes continue to shape advocacy practices. Today, one of the major tasks of advocates is assisting women in obtaining criminal and civil orders of protection. Many agencies have advocates permanently located at the courthouse. As with the antirape movement, in addition to providing services for abused women, prevention work has also become an important activity of battered women's agencies.

LINKING PAST AND PRESENT: SEXUAL ASSAULT AND DOMESTIC VIOLENCE SERVICES

Although each rape crisis center and domestic violence shelter has its unique organizational history, a remarkable similarity exists across agencies with respect to the services offered to victimized women and their families. Most centers and shelters have 24-hour crisis hotlines to provide information, referrals, and crisis counseling. In addition, most agencies have trained volunteers as legal and medical advocates to accompany victims to police departments, courtrooms, and hospitals. These volunteers provide information to victims about their legal rights and advocate on their behalf. Many agencies offer counseling and prevention education to the community. Influenced by the radical feminist women's movement, many centers and shelters actively support a social change agenda by sponsoring public demonstrations, protests, and marches as well as continued lobbying for stronger laws on violence against women.

Services for Victims of Sexual Assault

Current funding sources (e.g., state Victims of Crime Act funds) often require rape crisis centers to offer three basic services: (a) a 24-hour hotline; (b) counseling (individual, group, support groups); and (c) legal and medical advocacy. Crisis hotlines are typically staffed by volunteers who have completed an intensive training program in crisis intervention (Campbell et al., 1998). Crisis hotlines are open 24 hours a day, 7 days a week. Women who have been assaulted and their friends, family, and significant others can speak to advocates about abuse experiences and get resources to address specific issues such as counseling. The counseling services to help women (and sometimes their family members and significant others) address the violence they've experienced are commonly provided by licensed professionals (e.g., MSW-level practitioners), although some centers still employ paraprofessionals for short-term counseling and support group facilitation (Campbell et al., 1998). A critical element of the counseling work in these settings is understanding sexual assault from the perspective of power and control and gender inequality. This perspective also shapes the prevention activities that many agencies offer to schools and the community, important services that draw from the movements' original mission of gender equality and social change. In prevention education, agencies debunk sexual assault myths, deconstruct gender roles, conduct legal education, and teach safety strategies.

Of the three basic services (i.e., hotline, counseling, and advocacy) legal and medical advocacy remain the most challenging tasks for rape crisis center staff (Campbell, 1996; Martin, 1997). Rape victim advocates have the simultaneous job of assisting rape survivors in crisis and educating staff from other service systems (e.g., police officers, detectives, prosecutors, doctors, and nurses). Throughout all aspects of their work, rape victim advocates are trying to prevent "the second rape"—insensitive, victim-blaming treatment from community system personnel. Also termed "secondary victimization," victims may experience negative treatment after the rape that mirrors and exacerbates the trauma of the rape (Campbell, 1998; Campbell & Bybee, 1997; Campbell, Sefl, et al., 1999; Frohmann, 1991; Madigan & Gamble, 1991; Martin & Powell, 1994; Matoesian, 1993; Williams, 1984).

Medical-legal advocates typically are volunteers who have completed a comprehensive training program to assist victims in accessing emergency medical services and reporting the assault to the police. The process of reporting and prosecuting a rape may be long and complicated and, in fact, most rape victims never report the assault

(Campbell, Sefl, et al., 1999; Golding, Siegel, Sorenson, Burnam, & Stein, 1989; Ullman, 1996). The first contact, for those who do report, is with police officers and detectives, who record victims' accounts of the assault and conduct a preliminary investigation. Jurisdictions vary in whether this report-investigation will automatically be forwarded to the prosecutor or if the police decide whether to forward the report. The prosecutor then chooses whether to authorize an arrest and press charges. Not all cases are charged as rapes or sexual assaults, as some are charged at lesser offenses (e.g., simple assault, reckless endangerment). If the charges are not dropped, the accused rapist has the choice of pleading guilty to the original offense or, if a bargain has been struck, to a lesser offense, or going to trial. If he is convicted at the trial, the judge or jury must decide whether probation or jail time will suffice as punishment.

With a system this complex, it is quite likely that some cases will never be addressed and, in fact, most rape survivors never get their day in court. Only 25% of reported rapes are accepted for prosecution, 12% of defendants are found guilty, and 7% of all cases result in a prison term (Frazier & Haney, 1996). Even among survivors who had the assistance of a rape victim advocate, 67% had their legal cases dismissed and, more than 80% of the time, this decision was made by legal personnel and contradicted the victims' wishes to prosecute (Campbell, 1998). Thus, the effectiveness of RCCs' advocates can be limited because widespread effective prosecution of rape remains elusive.

In addition to providing legal advocacy, RCC staff also assist victims with their medical needs (see Martin & DiNitto, 1987; Martin, DiNitto, Harrison, & Maxwell, 1985). After a sexual assault, rape victims may need emergency medical care for several reasons. Victims are sometimes physically injured in the assault (e.g., cuts, bruises, vaginal or anal lacerations), so a medical exam is helpful to detect and treat these problems. In addition, forensic evidence such as semen, blood, or samples of hair, fiber, or skin may be collected from victims' bodies during this exam (often called the "rape kit"—see Martin et al., 1985). For many women, concern about exposure to sexually transmitted diseases (STDs) and the risk of pregnancy is paramount, and hospital staff may provide information and preventive treatments for these issues (e.g., the morning-after pill to prevent pregnancy). In practice, seeking medical care may be a harrowing experience for rape survivors: disrobing in front of the hospital staff, turning over their clothes to police as evidence, enduring a lengthy pelvic exam (to check for injuries and obtain semen samples), and submitting to other evidence collection (combing pubic hair, scraping under fingernails). In the midst of these procedures, nurses come and go taking blood (pregnancy, STD screening) and bringing medications (morning-after pill, antibiotics). This medical care is typically provided in a hospital emergency room, which, as a trauma-focused setting, can be quite frenetic (see Ahrens et al., 2000). The job of the medical advocate is to explain these medical procedures and help victims to restore their sense of control.

Current research suggests that many survivors are not receiving adequate care. The National Victim Center's (1992) national survey of female survivors of sexual assault found that 60% of victims were not advised about pregnancy testing or how to prevent pregnancy. Although 43% of the women who had been raped within the last five years were very concerned about contracting HIV from the assault, 73% were not given information about testing for exposure to HIV. Another 40% were not given information about the risk of contracting other sexually transmitted diseases. Yet, working with a RCC medical advocate appears to increase the likelihood of receiving needed medical services. Campbell and Bybee (1997) found that in a sample of rape survivors who had the assistance of an advocate, 67% of the victims who wanted information about STDs actually received such information from hospital staff. Similarly, 70% of the victims who wanted information about pregnancy obtained it, but only 38% of the victims who wanted the morning-after pill to prevent pregnancy actually received this medication, despite intensive efforts of the advocates. These results suggest that medical advocates are usually able to help rape victims obtain needed services.

Domestic Violence Services

Like rape crisis centers, domestic violence agencies typically provide a crisis hotline, counseling, and advocacy services. They also provide prevention education to the community. Similar to sexual assault services, crisis hotlines and medical and legal advocacy are typically staffed by volunteers who have received intensive training in crisis intervention and the legal procedures for acquiring an order of protection. The telephone crisis hotline operates 24 hours a day, 7 days a week. Abused women and their families, friends, and significant others can speak to hotline staff about the abuse experience and get resources to address specific issues such as counseling, housing, or childcare. Counseling services are usually administered by licensed professionals although, like RCCs, some agencies still employ paraprofessionals for short-term counseling and support group facilitation. Unlike most sexual assault programs, domestic violence agencies also provide housing and shelter for battered women and their children.

Shelters are a critical feature of services for battered women. They offer safe refuge for women and their children, providing time for women to think about their options and seek social, legal, and medical services if needed. General evaluations of shelter services suggest that these services are helpful to battered women. Berk, Newton, and Berk (1986) found that a shelter stay can reduce the frequency and intensity of new violence, but these effects depend on whether the woman had already begun to make changes in her life. When survivors of violence capitalized on the opportunities and services provided at a shelter, they experienced less severe abuse when they returned to the relationship. Similarly, Campbell, Sullivan, and Davidson (1995) found that after staying in a shelter, women were less depressed and more hopeful. Although shelter services are clearly important to battered women, much of the evaluation research has focused on advocacy programs.

Battered women's advocacy services began when shelter staff, sometimes survivors of battering themselves, accompanied and supported women as they navigated the legal, medical, and social systems seeking protection from future abuse. Advocates fill the gap between women seeking assistance and institutional agents who may not be sympathetic. In a two-year follow-up of the effectiveness of advocacy services, Sullivan and Bybee (1999) found that women who worked with advocates experienced less violence and had better access to community resources than women who did not receive advocacy. Advocates also use the knowledge gained from individual advocacy to challenge institutions' policies, procedures, and laws. This work is known as systems advocacy.

One of the primary areas in which advocacy occurs is the legal system. Here, individual advocates educate women about the legal process, legal terminology, and available options. They also may provide transportation to the court or other agencies. Legal systems advocacy includes the education of police and judges and other court personnel about battering and battering laws, developing new police and prosecutor protocols for battered women, and developing new legislation responsive to battered women and their needs (Sullivan, Tan, Basta, Rumptz, & Davidson, 1992).

The importance of advocacy for abused women cannot be underestimated. Hart found that outreach by advocates "often facilitates victim participation in and commitment to the criminal justice process" (Hart, 1993, p. 630). Working with advocates, battered women learn about the criminal justice system within a supportive context, and women who receive advocacy services are more likely to seek and follow through with legal remedies (Weisz, 1999; Weisz, Tolman, & Bennett, 1998).

Advocacy is not limited to the criminal justice system. Agencies also provide social service advocacy and medical advocacy. In examining general advocacy, Sullivan et al. (1992) report that women who received intensive advocacy services in shelters were more effective in achieving their goals than those who did not receive these services. Sullivan and Bybee's (1999) recent research reports the importance of advocacy services for battered women's safety and quality of life. They followed women who received 10 weeks of intensive advocacy services for two years at six-month intervals. The advocates worked with women to identify their unmet needs and help them access community resources. Over the two-year follow-up period, 24% of women who worked with advocates experienced no physical abuse by the original assailant or a new partner, compared to 10% of women who had not received advocacy services. Women who participated in the advocacy program made long-term improvements in their lives. Specifically, they had higher levels of social support, obtained more of the resources they sought, had fewer depressive symptoms, and were more effective at acquiring social support than those in the control group.

As noted above, battered women's agencies have also expanded their services to include counseling and prevention education. Counseling services provide women and their children with the skills to address the violence in their lives. Counseling services are usually offered individually as well as in support group settings. Like sexual assault counseling, domestic violence counseling explores battering from the perspective of power, control, and gender inequality. A review of nine studies of psychosocial, supportive counseling for battered women found mostly positive results, with improved emotional well-being and self-esteem and, in some cases, reductions in violence (Abel, 2000).

Prevention work done by domestic violence agencies in the schools and community also focuses on power and gender inequality. Prevention education works with community members to identify the cycle of violence in battering relationships, debunk battering myths, and help women and men develop nonviolent methods of conflict resolution.

Addressing Issues of Diversity

The violence against women's movement has worked hard over the last 30 years to make the medical, legal, and social systems more responsive to abused and assaulted women. In spite of this change, the movement has not always been able to achieve one of its initial goals: to be inclusive and welcoming of all women. The mainstream violence against women movement is comprised primarily of white middle-class women. Women of color, lesbians, and poor women are continually challenging the violence against women social movement organizations to attend to needs of diverse populations of victimized women. Some women outside the mainstream who have worked in agencies and those who have received services from these agencies report feeling invisible, tokenized, betrayed, dismissed, and erased from mainstream women's history and activism (Chow, 1989; Moraga & Anzaldua, 1981; Richie, 2000). To address the unmet needs within the African American, Latino, Asian, and Native American communities, women have developed services grounded in the multidimensionality of women of color's everyday lives. Organizations such as the Institute of Domestic Violence in the African American Community have been established to support these efforts.

The work by feminists of color alerted the mainstream violence against women movement that many of the strategies put forward to address issues of sexual assault and battering do not recognize the realities in communities of color. For instance, one of the primary strategies has been to challenge the criminal justice response to the crimes of violence against women. This ongoing work has made it possible for women to look to the court and police for intervention without being mistreated, dismissed, or blamed for the violence. On the other hand, the criminalization of rape and battery and push for prosecution and increased sentences for perpetrators have made communities of color somewhat ambivalent. Historically and currently the police, courts, and prisons have been agencies of repression in these communities. Davis (1985) noted that there is a long-standing history of harming people of color to protect the legal interests of white people, including the raping of slave women by their masters, creating false accusations of rape against black men to justify lynching, and the raping of Native women as a tool of war and genocide. In addition, research on the police responses to violence against women documents that the fear of police has been a major reason women of color, especially immigrant women, do not contact police for assistance (Abraham, 2000; Crenshaw, 1994; Ferraro, 1989a, 1989b; Jang, Lee, & Frosch, 1990; Narayan, 1995).

For many immigrant women, the marginalization from the women's movement has been even greater than for some women of color. Language barriers prevent women from socializing outside the community, separating them from access to information and support services that could provide assistance. Furthermore, in many cultures, the role of women is to be subservient and care for men and children. Such norms go a long way in denying the existence of battering and maintaining the illusion that women are well-treated within the family. Women do not want to bring shame on their families, themselves, or their community, so they remain silent. In addition, U.S. immigration law requirements for permanent residency status make it difficult for women to leave an abusive relationship without jeopardizing their status in the country. Immigrant women are often reluctant to call the police because of fear of deportation of themselves or their husbands (Crenshaw, 1994; Erez, 2000; Narayan, 1995).

As a result, women of color in the antiviolence movements have called for a broader definition of violence, one that integrates both personal and state violence in response to violence against women (Davis, 2000; Smith, 2001). Broadening the definition of violence against women, expanding the image of assaulted and battered women beyond the white middle-class community, and developing policies, procedures, and laws that recognize the life experiences of all women are critical for the success of the violence against women movement as a whole.

Limited integration within the movement has also had an effect on service provision. For example, agencies often have a limited ability to provide multilingual services and shelter staff may not have the training to address the needs of diverse women (the gaps in service provision are also affected by lack of funding). Although agencies are working hard to address the different cultural and religious needs of their clients, gaps remain.

For evaluators who are unfamiliar with the sexual assault and domestic violence movements, understanding their histories and current concerns as well as the lives of their clients is essential in order to tailor an evaluation to reflect the agency being evaluated.

EMERGING DEMANDS FOR PROGRAM EVALUATION OF RAPE CRISIS CENTERS AND DOMESTIC VIOLENCE SHELTERS

Over the past 20 years, the use of program evaluation has become a major component of social services in the United States. Espoused as a tool for social policy decision making, the press for evaluation can be found in such diverse fields as health care, mental health services, crime control, and education. Program evaluation is rooted in applied domains of science (and provides policymakers with scientifically credible information about the effectiveness of social service initiatives). Advocates of program evaluation argue that social policy decisions must be based on valid evidence that programs work and, through the empirical techniques of evaluation science, we will be able to improve our responses to major social problems.

In addition to this interest in scientific policy making, program evaluation has become a widespread method for demonstrating accountability to funders and the public at large. Chronically tight budgets have produced an ever-increasing demand to gain maximum efficiency out of government expenditures. As a result, many funders— both government and private—are formally requiring program evaluation of the services they support. Competition between advocacy groups for their "fair share" of funds has intensified and it is no longer sufficient to provide well-articulated pleas for social programs. To be accountable to the public, policy officials are increasingly demanding evaluation of programs in order to support continued funding. Thus, program evaluation may provide policymakers with both scientific evidence of best practices as well as justification for the expenditures supporting such programs. (For further discussion on the use of evaluation for evidence-based practice, see Chapter 3.)

At the same time that program evaluation has become a driving force in service design and policy making, violence against women has become recognized as one of today's major social problems. The most visible change agents of the movement, the programs offered by rape crisis centers and domestic violence shelters, have gained credibility and their programs are being "mainstreamed" into social institutions such as the education, medical, mental health, and criminal justice systems. Therefore, it is not surprising that within the past five years, the press for evaluation in rape crisis centers and domestic violence shelters has steadily increased. For example, the federal Violence Against Women Act of 1994 stipulated formal evaluation of the programs funded by this initiative. Expectations for evaluation extend beyond major federal initiatives: Local centers and shelters are increasingly being asked to demonstrate the effectiveness of their efforts (Campbell & Martin, 2001).

Requirements for evaluation have not been uniformly well received by violence against women social service agencies (Campbell & Martin, 2001; Riger, 1999). The antirape and battered women's social movements have had a long-standing conflicted relationship with government funding agencies (Byington et al., 1991, Campbell et al., 1998; Gornick et al., 1985; Koss & Harvey, 1991; Martin et al., 1992; Matthews, 1994). Many rape crisis centers and domestic violence shelters were created through grassroots efforts and volunteer labor (Campbell et al., 1998; Koss & Harvey, 1991; Riger, 1994; Schechter, 1982). The founding philosophies of such violence against women agencies emphasized nonhierarchical organizational structures that shared decision-making power and service delivery duties between volunteers, staff, and clients. Yet, as the demand for services provided by these agencies has increased, many rape crisis centers and domestic violence shelters have turned to government and other funding sources to expand their programs. The acceptance of funds often binds these agencies to the rules and regulations of their funders. Top-down funder-enforced evaluations may be perceived by rape crisis center or shelter staff as an intrusive, unhelpful presence that does not improve their services but rather detracts scarce time and resources from service delivery.

Evaluating the services provided by rape crisis centers and domestic violence shelters may in some cases undermine the goal of those services. Evaluation of victim services poses particular challenges with respect to safety and confidentiality of the clients served (see Sullivan, 1998). In some respects, the methods and techniques of program evaluation may clash with the needs of rape survivors and battered women. For example:

1. For some agencies, the idea of administering evaluation runs counter to their advocate mission. These agencies define their role as providing unconditional support for clients, no questions asked. Asking for nothing in return is one of the ways they distinguish themselves from social service or law enforcement agencies. Doing evaluation by questioning clients about services, for example, is asking them for something in return. It runs counter to the agencies' mission and violates their service principles.

2. Many women who receive services are in a state of immediate crisis and need. It may be unethical or impractical to ask victims in crisis to fill out a survey or participate in an interview to assess the effectiveness of a program.

3. In providing services to victimized women, staff and volunteers must work very hard to establish trusting, caring relationships with the victims of abuse. Asking clients to participate in a program evaluation during a period of trust building may jeopardize these relationships.

4. At any stage during victims' recovery process, it can be difficult to collect evaluation information from survivors without appearing intrusive.

5. It is difficult and potentially unethical to follow up with victims of abuse for evaluative purposes. Contacting clients via mail or phone may place them in danger. Contacting clients many months after an assault might be an unwelcome reminder of what they have gone through.

Mandated program evaluations that are not attentive to these challenges will not likely gain the support of center staff; most important, they may compromise the safety of the participants.

Although it is quite possible to design and implement program evaluations that address the specific needs of survivors of abuse, such efforts may require more resources than these small local organizations can realistically afford. Program evaluation requires scientific and administrative resources, which may be beyond the reach of individual rape crisis centers and domestic violence shelters. Not all funding agencies that require program evaluation also provide the resources needed to conduct such efforts. Therefore, it is not uncommon for violence against women social service agencies to face mandated evaluation with very little support. In response to this dilemma, Edleson and Frick (1997) developed a comprehensive resource guide for evaluation of domestic violence services that can be used by small, local shelters. Since then, other researchers and advocates have developed similar evaluation protocols (e.g., Sullivan, 1998). Yet, ongoing consultation and support throughout the entire evaluation process remain a pressing need.

Thus, the extent to which program evaluation is friend or foe, consistent or inconsistent with the values of the violence against women social movement, depends on the model used for such evaluation. Approaches that respect the independence and autonomy of service agencies, respond to the specific safety, confidentiality, and recovery needs of victims of abuse, and provide ongoing support and resources may be quite helpful to both service providers and policymakers. Most important, they may help improve services to victims of abuse.

KEY POINTS

- The violence against women movement emerged from the larger movement of second-wave feminism in the 1970s.
- Although the antirape and antibattering movements overlap, they have distinct histories.
- Some women of color and immigrant women have felt tokenized, excluded, and ignored by the mainstream (white, middle-class)

violence against women movement. Some policies have not been sensitive to life experiences of women of color.

- Women of color have developed strategies that call for a broader definition of violence against women that is inclusive of both personal and political–state violence. They have adopted a methodological and theoretical approach that recognizes the multidimensional quality of people's lives and developed policies from this perspective.
- The primary services offered by sexual assault service providers are a rape crisis hotline, advocacy, and counseling. Many agencies also do prevention education.
- The primary services offered by the domestic violence agencies are advocacy, shelter, and counseling. Many agencies also provide a crisis hotline and prevention education services.
- Sexual assault agencies and battered women's shelters are increasingly being asked to engage in formal evaluation processes by funders.
- Agencies may perceive funder requests for evaluation as intrusive and a diversion of valuable resources from service delivery. The structure of formalized program evaluation may conflict with feminist advocacy philosophy and the nonhierarchical organization structure of agencies. Evaluating the services provided by rape crisis centers and domestic shelters may, in some cases, undermine the goal of those services or appear inconsistent with survivors' needs.
- To conduct a helpful evaluation, the evaluator should choose approaches that respect the independence and autonomy of service agencies, respond to the specific safety, confidentiality, and recovery needs of victims of abuse, and provide ongoing support and resources.

2

Collaboration in Evaluation Research

Evaluation of domestic violence and sexual assault services often requires collaboration among practitioners, researchers with evaluation skills, and funding agencies. All of these groups have much to gain by working together. Practitioners may benefit from the expertise and effort of researchers, and researchers with evaluation skills welcome the opportunity to collect data at service delivery agencies. Researchers may develop scientific knowledge and may help answer practice-driven questions whereas practitioners may use research findings to improve services, impress funders, and change policies and public opinion.

Collaborations occur not only because these groups benefit but also because funders and others increasingly mandate collaboration. Several funding agencies, such as the Centers for Disease Control and the National Institute of Justice, require collaboration in research on domestic violence. Many research projects must have advisory boards of community members and some innovative service projects require an evaluation component.

But even if we collaborate because we want to, not just because we have to, tensions may arise in the relationship between researchers and practitioners. More than 30 years ago, when many grassroots programs that respond to violence against women began, researchers and practitioners were fairly distinct in interests and expertise. Today, however, many advocates and service providers have research training and many researchers have experience as advocates. Although they overlap considerably, even to the point where, in some cases, one person may occupy both roles, some place primacy on research whereas others give priority to service provision or advocacy. Therefore, for purposes of discussion, we portray researchers and practitioners as distinct groups.

Although they may share the common goal of ending violence against women, researchers and practitioners may differ in their priorities. Researchers may be most interested in developing knowledge and theories; practitioners may be more concerned with social action (Chavis, Stucky, & Wandersman, 1983; Nyden & Wiewel, 1992). Typically, practitioners and researchers (especially those in academic settings) work in organizations with different cultures. Researchers may be rewarded for publications with promotions and research funding. To practitioners, such rewards may be irrelevant. To them, successful research is that which benefits their communities and promotes social change. Practitioners and researchers may differ somewhat in their professional backgrounds and expertise and they use different terminology (Gondolf, Yllö, & Campbell, 1997; Jacobson, 1994). Moreover, differences in race, class, gender, and sexual orientation between practitioners and researchers (and within each group) may exacerbate mistrust (Renzetti, 1997). These differences may produce tensions that make it difficult to work together.

Collaborative research (also known as participatory research) has a long history in social science (see Cancian, 1993; Hall, 1992; Petras & Porpora, 1993) and studies on violence against women often use feminist collaborative research approaches (e.g., Renzetti, 1997). Collaboration in evaluation may range from joint development of research goals, methods, and interpretations of findings to occasional consultation with community representatives by researchers or even simply a researcher's request for a letter of support from practitioners. Yet a hallmark of collaborative research on violence against women is the desire to share control of the research process and to involve all participants (be they researchers, advocates or service providers, community representatives, or women who have been abused) in many phases of research, from designing the research questions to collecting data to disseminating findings.

Several sources of tension may cause problems in the process of working together.

TRUST

Researchers who come into a community, collect data, and leave, doing what some call "drive-by data collection," have created a legacy of mistrust among community members. This kind of research may be exploitive, benefiting only the researcher and giving nothing back to the community. At its worst, it harms women if the research is designed or interpreted in ways that "blame the victim," is inaccurate, or does not consider the safety and confidentiality of the participants. For these good reasons, some practitioners mistrust researchers.

Practitioners also fear harm to their programs from the results of evaluation research. Will an evaluation be done "with the project or 'to' the project" (Levin, 1999)? That is, are program staff to be involved in the design of the study and interpretation of data or will research "experts" collect data that they (unilaterally) deem important and interpret (or possibly misinterpret)? Today, with so much competition for funds, many people worry that any hint of negativity about a program may be used against it. A negative evaluation may enhance researchers' reputations for rigor but hasten the demise of a program (Lundy, Massat, Smith, & Bhasin, 1996). Evaluation researchers who are not sensitive to the political environment in which a program exists inadvertently may provide fuel for its enemies. At the same time, practitioners need to be willing to acknowledge that their programs might not be achieving the desired outcomes. Especially when dealing with violence, confidentiality and safety of clients are of utmost concern.

Practitioners may fear that researchers will not be sensitive to these issues or that the process of participating in a research interview will create anxiety or distress (Gondolf et al., 1997). However, clients may benefit from the opportunity to tell their stories and opinions to researchers (Hutchinson, Wilson, & Wilson, 1994; Lundy et al., 1996), and innovative data collection techniques can protect women's privacy. For example, a study of domestic violence suffered by women on welfare used tape recorders to ensure privacy while conducting interviews in busy welfare offices. Women listened through headphones to questions about domestic violence on a prerecorded tape and marked their responses on an answer sheet that contained only question numbers and response categories. This technique not only enabled women to respond privately but it also overcame literacy problems (Lennett & Colten, 1999); with sufficient resources, it could be adapted to evaluation research. A feminist researcher in another study argued successfully against the use of tape recorders in interviews with abused women, claiming that mechanical devices would heighten women's suspicion and fear of being interviewed (Gondolf et al., 1997). Tape recorders worked well in the first setting, a relatively public office of a state agency, but they were not appropriate in the second situation, private interviews with women who had just given birth. Although they adopted opposite strategies, both studies tailored their research methods to meet the specific needs of the women being interviewed, based on advice from practitioners.

Another source of mistrust, not only between practitioners and researchers but also within each group, may lie in the clashing assumptions that people hold about violence against women. Some assumptions stem from an individualistic perspective about the causes of violence as well as areas to target for intervention or treatment. This perspective assumes that causes for action lie within the individual and often ignores the role of social context in shaping behavior. Research done from this perspective, such as that which seeks to identify characteristics of women likely to be battered, isolates women from factors in their environment, such as racism or class discrimination, that may affect their responses to violence. In so doing, this research may imply that women are responsible for their abuse (Fine, 1989). Working with practitioners who are aware of the importance of contextual factors may counter this individualistic bias. This may be particularly important in evaluating the impact of services so that services are judged according to the intended outcomes. For example, in the process of developing a measure of counseling outcomes for domestic violence programs in Illinois, practitioners suggested the addition of an item stating that clients understand that domestic violence is a social problem, not an individual fault. This item reflected the practitioners' perspective on violence and was incorporated into their work with clients. Omitting this item would have ignored an important underpinning of their programs.

Unforeseen events may occur that exacerbate tensions and require partners to renegotiate their understandings and working procedures. For example, two months into the year-long evaluation of domestic violence and sexual assault services in Illinois, the university housing the evaluation research team suspended all of its research activities because of violations in procedures protecting the safety of subjects. Even though those violations occurred in other studies and had nothing to do with this evaluation project, the researchers, as members of the university, were prohibited temporarily from doing research. Agencies could continue to collect evaluation data (because they were collecting it for the state funding agency, not the university), but the researchers could not touch those data until their project was reapproved under stringent new guidelines for the protection of research participants. The reapproval process took six months because the university had to revamp its procedures for training researchers and approving projects. A great deal of time was lost and relationships between the evaluators and some agencies were strained because of this delay. Unanticipated events are likely to happen in any evaluation and may exacerbate existing tensions between collaborators.

Overcoming distrust between researchers and advocates (or within each group) is not simply a matter of good communication or whether researchers are "good" people who don't exploit. It also is a matter of power and control.

POWER AND CONTROL

Evaluation may be done voluntarily, because an agency decides it will be worthwhile, or it may be mandated by funders or others. In the latter case, agencies may resent their lack of control and resist the evaluation process. Researchers working in this situation need to be especially sensitive to the concerns of service providers if the evaluation is to succeed.

Questions of control of an evaluation are particularly delicate because researchers may be connected with relatively resource-rich universities whereas advocates often come from small, underfunded community agencies. Rarely do community organizations have the resources to pay for and, thus perhaps control, researchers. If additional funding is obtained to conduct an evaluation, power struggles may be reflected in conflict over who controls that funding. Developing trusting relationships may create a context in which power differentials are negotiated but trust does not negate these inequalities (Lykes, 1989). These issues are especially difficult with respect to evaluation research when a program's future funding (or even its existence) may depend, at least in part, on the outcome of an evaluation. Resolving questions of power is often the most difficult aspect of collaboration (Altman, 1995).

Several questions arise in the course of collaborating on an evaluation.

Whose priorities will predominate? Researchers may be concerned with theory development or with the collection of data whereas practitioners may be less concerned about theory than they are with the need for answers to immediate questions or with the well-being of participants in the study (Altman, 1995). The emotional or safety needs of women who have been abused may at times conflict with the data collection process. Evaluating a rape crisis hotline service ideally may be done with a follow-up phone call to clients some time after the crisis call. However, this would require obtaining callers' names and phone numbers, something that may violate their confidentiality or even their safety.

One way to deal with this dilemma is to train interviewers in advocacy and to train advocates to interview so that researchers are familiar with domestic violence and sexual assault issues and practitioners are familiar with evaluation research. For example, interviewers in a crime-related study became concerned about how to respond to women who had been raped. The interviewers did not want to be placed in the role of counselor, yet they wanted to respond to women's needs. The solution was to have the interviewer give the respondent a list of local rape victim resources, ask her if she was familiar with them, and leave the list with her (Gordon & Riger, 1989). A similar compromise was reached in a study of battered women who had just given birth. Some researchers wanted the women to be interviewed by tape recorder or at least by interviewers who were unaware of the purpose of the research whereas feminist advocates insisted that the interviewers be formerly battered women who could empathize and intervene in battering situations. The solution was to train advocates in interview techniques and to have them use a structured interview. The advocates were able to offer support and information when appropriate (Gondolf et al., 1997).

A difficulty occurs, however, if the advocates who are collecting evaluation data are the same people who have delivered services to clients. Clients may give a favorable evaluation out of fear of losing services, to be responsive to the service provider, or for other reasons not related to the quality of the services. Providing services and also asking questions evaluating those services may be difficult for service providers for another reason. Many are trained in an empowerment model. This model seeks to reinstate women's control of their lives after they have experienced violence. Asking evaluation questions may be seen as interfering with a client's control of an interaction and thus working against the service providers' goals. Providers may see conducting the evaluation as acting for the benefit of the agency rather than client.

Who decides how the study is going to be done? Conflicts may surface in the process of deciding about the design of an evaluation project. For example, in evaluating interventions, conflict may occur over the use of a control group of women who do not receive the new program (Gondolf et al., 1997). From a research perspective, control groups may be essential in order to determine if the program has an impact; from a practitioner's viewpoint, denying participation in an effective program is unethical. Ways to resolve this dilemma include giving the control group the new program after the study is done (requiring that funding or other support for the intervention also include resources to carry out the program with the control group at a later date). But issues like this raise the question of which gets priority: research or service concerns (Altman, 1995)?

Who owns the data? That is, who gets to use the data and for what purpose (e.g., for publicity, advocacy, scientific publications)? A study of violence against women who were receiving public aid came up with a unique solution to this question. The collaborators developed two separate reports based on the research. The researchers' report presented the survey methodology and findings whereas the advocates' report suggested policy directions based on those findings (Lennett & Colten, 1999). In this way, the researchers were able to maintain their preferred role as neutral fact finders while advocates addressed the implications for policy.

If the researchers and advocates disagree about interpretation of the data, whose interpretation will prevail? Differences may exist about the meaning of evaluation findings. At times, people may interpret research findings in strikingly different ways. A researcher, for example, studying corporate wives rejected their claims of contentment, attributing them to "false consciousness," a Marxist term meaning that these women identified with (male) ruling class interests against their own (female) class interests. The women wrote a rebuttal to the researcher rejecting her interpretation. In response, the researcher revised her position to accept the women's statements of satisfaction with their lives but looked for sources of their contentment in their position in the social hierarchy (Andersen, 1981).

This kind of dialogic process recognizes the viewpoint of the researcher but avoids imposing interpretations on research participants (Lather, 1986). Without such a dialogue, we grant privilege to the authority of the researcher. Yet such a dialogue must also recognize that those in different positions have different amounts of power. The issue, therefore, is not simply one of "different perspectives" but rather the unequal positions and the relations between them that shape those perspectives (Gorelick, 1991). That is, differences in perspective at times reflect dominance, or unequal power, positions. The views of researchers who write reports of an evaluation may predominate over service providers who may disagree but who are not involved in report writing and so have difficulty getting their views known.

One solution would be for evaluators to leave interpretation of data to programs themselves. For example, in the evaluation that we conducted in Illinois, we provided agencies (and funders) with the results of the evaluation (e.g., frequency scores and average responses to items on evaluation measures) but we did not interpret the meaning of those results. We did not, for instance, give our opinion about whether a certain score meant that an agency was doing well or poorly with respect to a specific service. Multiple factors affect the outcome of services and identifying those factors may be outside the scope of an evaluation. To illustrate, suppose that clients do not find legal advocacy helpful. That outcome may be due to poor performance by an advocate or it may be the result of a client's experience with a hostile judge. Practical limits to evaluation may prohibit asking additional questions that would enable determination of which interpretation is most accurate. In this case, agencies themselves may best be able to interpret findings. (We did give training in how to understand the numbers in our evaluation reports. See our Web site for further information: www.uic.edu/depts/psch/idhs.)

In a program evaluation, who defines success? For example, using reduction in violence as an indicator of success may be holding a program for women with abusive partners accountable for men's actions, which are beyond its control or influence (Gondolf et al., 1997; Sullivan, 1998). It is essential for evaluators to understand the goals (and obstacles toward achieving those goals) of domestic violence and sexual assault programs in order to evaluate those programs fairly. However, evaluators may also have to educate advocates about how to define measurable goals. For example, a rape crisis counseling program may have the goal of overcoming feelings of isolation and shame in the aftermath of being raped. A measurable objective of this larger goal might be that clients feel supported by their counselors. One way to assess this would be to ask clients how much support they felt they received from talking with a counselor. Researchers thus may help practitioners identify goals and translate them into measurable form.

The issues of power and control discussed above are not simply matters of trust or good communication; rather, they require a clear articulation of how control (and rewards) will be distributed among those working together and the development of a mechanism for making decisions when disagreement occurs. It may be tempting to attribute conflict to insufficient understanding or lack of commitment on the part of (other) participants, but conflict is inevitable in any work group, just as in any ongoing relationship. The absence of explicit mechanisms for dealing with conflict makes it difficult to negotiate disagreements openly, leaving a group vulnerable to control by its most forceful or well-connected members while others become frustrated or alienated (Riger, 1994).

TIME PERSPECTIVE

Researchers may take a long-term time perspective. They are trained to gather complete information on a topic. They want to take time to develop research instruments carefully and test them, sometimes repeatedly, until they are considered satisfactory. Furthermore, researchers know that the results of any one study are not likely to be conclusive; they are trained to consider the preponderance of evidence from a large number of studies. Advocates, on the other hand, often have to make quick decisions based on incomplete information (Altman, 1995). They want—and need—answers soon. Their time perspective thus may sharply contrast with that of researchers.

The pressing need for solutions to social problems may cause the adoption of policies or programs based on the findings of one or two evaluation studies when the conclusions of those studies may be called into question by subsequent research. For example, an influential study found that arresting men who were assaulting their wives or lovers led to a reduction in domestic violence (Sherman, 1992). Efforts by some advocates, supported by these findings, led to "mandatory arrest" laws in at least 17 states and the District of Columbia, which require police to make arrests when called to domestic assaults or when civil protection orders are violated. But a more recent study, done by the same researcher (Schmidt & Sherman, 1993), found that whether or not the men were employed made a critical difference in subsequent levels of violence. Among men who were employed, being arrested led to a decline in their rates of domestic violence in the year after being released from jail. But those who were unemployed were more likely to be violent if they had been arrested than if they had only been warned. Basing legal policy on a single study may have inadvertently raised the levels of violence against some women. Furthermore, the mandatory arrest laws may have had the unintended consequence of an increase in the number of women arrested for wounding men, even in self-defense.

Time is important for collaborative research in another way. The continuous negotiation required to maintain a successful collaborative relationship takes a great deal of time. As Edleson and Bible point out, "Negotiating the research design, implementation procedures, interpretation, and publication of results is extremely time-consuming in general, and is even more so when the process is shared among collaborators from different disciplines who often have different values" (2001, p. 76). Those for whom research is a central part of their jobs may have time to discuss research issues in detail. In contrast, for practitioners, research may be an addition to what is already a more than full-time job, giving them little time (except overtime) to collaborate with researchers. Public agencies may be especially crisis driven and pressed to respond to immediate needs (Lundy et al., 1996). Researchers can respect this by fitting their needs into advocates' existing schedules, for example, by attending regularly scheduled staff meetings rather than setting up additional meetings and in other ways organizing the research at the advocates' convenience.

Collaboration may become a long-term commitment that lasts beyond any particular project or its participants. Such a commitment to an ongoing relationship helps to overcome temporary conflicts. Yet maintaining long-term relationships takes time and effort. A study of battered women's risk of homicide included in its advisory group representatives of six agencies, four out-of-town consultants, and four local experts. This project used a variety of means including phone calls, faxes, e-mails, and letters to keep its advisory group members informed. The researchers distributed detailed minutes of meetings and found that some advisory board members who could not attend meetings would respond to queries that were included in the minutes. Some members would participate actively when their expertise was useful and not at other times. More than 20 people contributed to the development of the survey used in this project, but such wide participation required many months of effort. Keeping everyone familiar with the project's progress, and making sure that people received credit for their contributions, helped to maintain a large and diverse group over time (Block, Engel, Naureckas, & Riordan, 1999).

The time necessary for collaboration may have extra costs for some participants. Funders and administrators (such as academic review committees seeking a large quantity of publications from candidates for tenure) may be impatient with the time that relationship building requires (Wiewel & Lieber, 1998). Participatory research may retard academic publication and career advancement (Cancian, 1993; Israel, Schurman, & Hugentobler, 1992) or at least require that a researcher justify the added time necessary to do community research.

Time may also be a concern for programs collecting their own evaluation data. Practitioners may resent the time taken from service delivery that is necessary to fill out evaluation forms—and the forms themselves may add to the burden of paperwork demanded of agency staff. Evaluators should look closely at the data already being collected by agencies to see if those data may be adapted for evaluation purposes. The more evaluation data collection can be integrated into ongoing practices of an agency, the less burdensome—and more likely to be completed—it will be.

EXPERTISE

Experience as a practitioner and research training develop different forms of expertise. (Many who work on violence against women have occupied both roles, so in practice these forms of expertise often overlap.) Practitioners have a wealth of knowledge that they have developed through direct experience with battered and abused women. Their close, day-to-day work gives them a fine-grained knowledge of these women's lives. They are likely to be particularly aware of the way that culture and ethnicity affect responses to abuse and so they know how research instruments should be modified for particular groups of women. Because of their close involvement in women's lives, they are aware firsthand of cutting edge issues that have not yet surfaced in research and policy discussions. Furthermore, they often are knowledgeable about the politics surrounding policies concerning violence and abuse, such as which legislators will support funding for certain programs. Battered women also contribute to research and theory, for example, by specifying outcome variables and identifying strategies to implement research safely (Gondolf et al., 1997).

Research training prepares one to collect data, conduct statistical tests, draw inferences from data, and report findings. Those with research training know how to evaluate whether a finding is consistent with other studies and whether a study is scientifically sound. They know formal theories about violence and abuse, and they know how to use data to enter into theoretical and policy debates on a national level. Research may give voice to women and to a point of view, using data as support, and it may provide guidance for program development. Moreover, findings from research may be convincing to funders and others concerned with a program's effectiveness or legitimacy.

It is essential that various people involved in an evaluation respect each other's expertise and contributions. Working well together may necessitate a shift from the role of "expert" to that of "colearner" (Brown, 1995; Israel et al., 1992; Renzetti, 1997). Levin (1999) describes evaluation researchers as invited guests whereas another metaphor is that of translator or mediator, in which the researcher interprets the concerns of one group in terms that are understandable to another and helps to negotiate agreements. Partnership is still another metaphor for collaboration, implying that all parties benefit from the relationship (Campbell, Dienemann, Kub, & Wurmser, 1999; Gondolf et al., 1997). Whether colearner, invited guest, translator, or partner, each of these metaphors reframes roles from that of expert to one of a participant on equal terms in a joint enterprise.

EMOTIONAL STRESS

Violence against women generates stress for both practitioners and researchers. Working day after day with women who are bruised and battered takes a toll, as evidenced in the high turnover rate among service providers. Researchers also find studying violence against women to be stressful. One project's staff stated that "constantly reading about and discussing rape and other forms of violence against women often left us anxious and depressed" (Gordon & Riger, 1989, p. xiii). Stanko (1997, p. 75) describes "anger, frustration, fear, and pain" during her research experiences whereas Moran-Ellis (1996, p. 181) uses the phrase "pain by proxy" to describe her emotional responses to her research on child sexual abuse. One benefit of collaboration is that experienced advocates may share with researchers strategies for coping with their own emotional distress (Lennett & Colten, 1999).

From a practitioner's perspective, evaluators may appear to have the luxury of separating themselves from immediate involvement with violence, even if they spend some time in a setting that serves abused women. Service providers who work in a shelter or who staff crisis lines may not have the same opportunity to leave violence behind while they work. They may resent what they perceive to be evaluators' relative freedom from the issue of violence. And researchers may have difficulty recognizing the emotional drain of doing such practice day after day, or they may find that their concern with violence against women separates them from peers doing research on more benign topics. Collaboration may reduce some of the isolation that contributes to stress for both groups (Gilfus, Fineran, Jensen, Cohan, & Hartwick, 1999).

Collaborative research paradigms bring special sources of tension for those trained in traditional research methods. Traditional positivist models of research separate thought from emotion, and reason from values (Saegert, 1993). Modeled after the physical sciences, traditional methods treat people being studied as objects and the researcher as the source of understanding and interpretation (Park, 1992). Collaborative models, in contrast, treat those who are studied as "experts" on themselves, abolishing the distinction between the knower and the known central to conventional research (Reason, 1993). For traditional researchers, the loss of control and authority implicit in a collaborative model may be unsettling. Those who are attracted to research because of its detached, analytic, intellectual nature may find that successful collaboration requires political and social skills that may not be part of researchers' professional training but that are necessary to develop relationships with nonresearchers (Nyden & Wiewel, 1992).

Gondolf et al. (1997) propose an "advocacy research" role that serves the concerns of practitioners much as a defense lawyer does a client. That is, the advocacy researcher uses research skills on behalf of practitioners and the battered women they represent rather than to promote a research agenda. Helping to refine concerns into researchable questions, explaining the advantages and disadvantages of various research designs, and discussing interpretations of findings with advocates are some functions that the advocacy researcher can fulfill. Yet an advocacy stance should not preclude using scientific strategies to minimize bias; criteria of reliability and validity still apply. Not addressing traditional concerns of rigorous science would mean that research is unlikely to be taken seriously by other researchers or funders.

In contrast to an advocacy research approach, Gelles (1994) argues that, "At best, researchers can use conceptual models and statistics about extent and correlation to inform clinicians and advocates. But those are the practical limits of research" (p. 95). In his view, researchers are "objective and dispassionate" truth seekers whereas advocates argue for their personal point of view. He claims that attempting to mix the two roles simultaneously is neither necessary nor productive.

The contrast between Gelles's position and that of advocacy research mirrors fundamental disagreements in science about objectivity. An advocacy research model, in which researchers' values are explicit, counters the positivist assumptions of research as value free. Feminists and others have argued that even traditional research is not value free (see Riger, 1992). Indeed, the very topics that researchers choose to explore reflect their beliefs and values. Recognizing the value-laden nature of research may be difficult to accept for those trained in the positivist model and imbued with its stance of objectivity. Two prominent researchers on violence against women reflect this struggle in referring to themselves as a "recovering positivist" (Koss, 1998) and "reformed positivist" (Renzetti, 1997).

CONCLUSION

Collaborative research evaluating services for abused women presents some special problems. High-quality, accurate research is especially important because of the imminent threat of harm to those who are the subjects of study. Moreover, the policy implications of research findings mean that it is critical that research not be "victim blaming," holding women responsible for men's actions that are not in women's control.

Jacobson (1994) describes dialogues on woman abuse that range from "stimulating intellectual discourse between camps with distinct but reconcilable world views to a downright hostile shouting match between advocates of seemingly contradictory positions" (p. 81). Shouting matches seem unlikely to help abused women. Practitioners and researchers may share a desire to end violence against women, yet, too often, each group considers the other to be antagonistic.

On the basis of four in-depth case studies of successful collaboration, Edleson and Bible (2001) recommend that researchers spend time with practitioners, that they share decision-making power, and that they help shape practitioners' concerns into researchable questions. Some researchers may work as volunteers in a program and eventually be considered "one of them." But other models of successful collaboration are possible. Despite the recent push to identify "best practices," several factors mitigate against one "best" way to collaborate.

First, the ecology of settings varies greatly. Resources, expertise, demand, and other factors differ considerably across locales, making each setting somewhat unique. Moreover, participants may interpret phenomena in varying ways. For example, researchers may see themselves as performing a useful service for practitioners; on the contrary, practitioners may see those same researchers as exploitative. Practitioners may view procedures for safeguarding participants in research as essential whereas those same procedures may seem excessively burdensome to researchers. Reaching common understandings and agreements requires establishing relationships, a process that may vary depending on the participants, their history, and numerous other factors. Consequently, no single collaboration strategy may best fit all settings.

One way to enhance the success of collaboration is to articulate expectations and goals as fully as possible before the research begins. Then, once a project begins, create a decision-making structure that makes explicit each person's responsibilities, areas of control, and rewards. Too often, the structural arrangements between researchers and advocates are left vague, open to varying interpretations by different people (Gondolf et al., 1997). Addressing sources of tension before the research begins will reduce some possibilities for conflict. For example, how and by whom will decisions get made about the research design? How will the data be reported? How will women's safety and confidentiality be ensured?

Participants in a collaborative evaluation project may not always be aware of all of their expectations and goals at the beginning of the project, and those goals may change over time. Despite preliminary agreements, therefore, issues will need to be renegotiated as research progresses. As in any continuing relationship, renegotiation of roles and obligations is constant (e.g., Renzetti, 1997). What may be predictable, however, is that conflict will inevitably arise and that some mechanism for dealing with conflict will be needed.

Moreover, conflict within collaboration may serve a useful purpose. As Fine (1992) claims, "The strength of feminist activist research lies in its ability to open contradictions within collaborative practices" (p. 220). The varying perspectives of different stakeholders are not only sources of disagreement and tension, they are also reflections of the ways people's position in a social system shapes their consciousness. As such, they become useful indicators of underlying processes; that is, the conflicts themselves are data about the phenomena of interest.

To sustain collaborative projects, we need forums in which we can begin to identify these conflicts, explore areas of agreement, and negotiate disagreement. Only by such continuing efforts will the potential of collaborative research be fully realized. The benefits of collaboration are many, including improved research designs and more effective services. Despite its many challenges, collaboration may be the best way to develop meaningful research findings that address the impact of services for domestic violence and sexual assault survivors.

KEY POINTS

- Collaboration in evaluation research produces tensions between practitioners and evaluators, although both groups have much to gain by working together.
- Practitioners may fear that the data collection process or the results of an evaluation will harm their programs or clients.
- Decisions about the design of the evaluation and distribution and interpretation of the findings may bring to the surface power and control conflicts between participants in an evaluation.
- Limited time and resources needed for an evaluation may exacerbate conflicts.

- Evaluation researchers and practitioners differ in their expertise; mutual respect is essential for a collaboration to succeed.
- Working on violence against women may be emotionally stressful for both practitioners and evaluators.
- Participants in a collaborative evaluation project would benefit from clarifying their goals and obligations at the beginning of the project as well as having a means to renegotiate their agreement as the research progresses.

PART II:
Key Aspects of Doing
an Evaluation

3

Why Evaluate?

In this chapter, we will discuss several reasons why agencies should evaluate the effects their services have on clients and a few reasons why agencies should *not* evaluate their services. We will talk about the motives for evaluating domestic violence and sexual assault programs as well as several conflicts that may sometimes arise from divergent motives. We will argue that the overriding reason to conduct an evaluation is accountability: to the people we try to help as well as to our communities. Recognizing that evaluations take place in a variety of settings for a variety of reasons, we will briefly present alternative and emergent approaches to evaluation in addition to traditional approaches. When discussing alternative and emergent approaches, we will present them not as conflicting but as compatible with traditional approaches. As part of our discussion of alternative approaches to evaluation, we will suggest that evaluators may also consider the impact of programs on the community as well as on the individual. Although most program funders think about changes in individuals as the unit of interest, domestic violence and sexual assault programs may also consider changes in the larger community as an equally important outcome of their work.

REASONS TO EVALUATE

The motivation to evaluate a sexual assault or domestic violence program may originate in a number of places. Institutions within the community, program staff, funders, or even participants of the program may all wonder about the effects a program has on those receiving services. Typically, requests for evaluation hinge on accountability to a funding source, a board of directors, or an external service network. The evaluation of sexual assault and domestic violence programs in Illinois that forms the basis for this book originated with a mandate from the Illinois Department of Human Services (DHS)—the primary funder of services for victims in Illinois—that all DHS-funded programs must collect standardized outcome data. Requests such as this will become increasingly common if, as expected, the trend toward evidence-based practice and accountability continues. Funding sources and governing boards alike want to know whether programs are doing what they said they would do, whether they are having the desired effects, and what the desired effects cost. Do women who use domestic violence agencies feel safer as a result of receiving services at the agency? Are the adverse effects of assault lessened by talking to rape victim advocates and counselors?

External requests for accountability from the community may spark frustration in agency staff who are struggling to provide badly needed services with scant resources. Funding agencies and governing boards are sometimes viewed by service providers as disinterested in the work of services to victims and interested only in the "bottom line": the cost of providing services. In some cases, agencies are required to document outcomes but given very little support for the evaluation process. Furthermore, some agencies have had experiences collecting and providing data for third parties who did not use the data after they were collected or who used the data for research that staff did not deem relevant to their clients' problems. Funders and outside evaluators must address these concerns if they are to gain trust and cooperation for evaluation from agencies.

As suggested, the interests of evaluators and practitioners are not always the same. Evaluators desire the consistent application of the intervention or program that is being evaluated because without such control it is difficult to understand exactly what is responsible for the program's outcomes. In order to find out what aspect of a program is responsible for its outcomes, researchers may want to control the delivery of the intervention and reduce a variety of extraneous factors that could affect outcome. If the delivery of the program varies from staff to staff, or from location to location, it is not possible to separate the effects of specific aspects of the program from the effects of staff or location differences. However, the consistency of an intervention is rarely the concern of practitioners. In fact, the skill of a practitioner may lie in the ability to improvise in the best interest of her or his clients, to add whatever additional supports and resources are necessary to ensure the well-being of the client she or he is helping.

Programs sometimes want their own evaluations, beyond the requests of funders and board members. Program staff often want to develop and improve their program and they may view evaluation as a tool that can assist them in doing so. Staff are concerned about providing the best service possible and are usually interested in knowing about best practice, or "what works." Knowing what works is also important to program administrators, particularly in those agencies that have developed beyond grassroots organizations. The transition from a grassroots community organization to a professionalized social service agency may be punctuated by a request for program evaluation. Regardless of whether such evolution to professionalization is desirable, it often brings with it a desire to establish the effectiveness of services.

Practitioners may believe they know what works. This may be based on their experience seeing victims become survivors while getting help from their agency, other experiences in similar settings, philosophical beliefs about the right thing to do in a given circumstance, personal experience of their own survival, or techniques they have learned in workshops, books, or courses. These are all legitimate ways of knowing what works. Program evaluation does not seek to eliminate these sources of knowledge but rather seeks to provide a systematic description of the factors associated with success for most people in the program. Traditional program evaluation improves on—but does not replace—these other forms of knowledge. Typically, the improvement is based on using research methods to systematically measure the effects of the program as well as factors other than the program that could account for the observed changes in clients.

Another motivation for program evaluation is concern about the unexpected effects of a program or the unexpected characteristics of program clients. For example, as domestic violence shelters became better established, staff found they were assisting women with far greater needs than the women they had helped in their early days in basements and walk-in centers. As public support for disenfranchised populations has declined over the past decade, battered women's agencies have increasingly found themselves serving a population they did not originally set out to serve. Shelters for battered women now provide a niche for homeless, mentally ill, and substance abusing women who are also victims of domestic abuse and who are not adequately served by homeless agencies, mental health centers, and substance abuse programs. Staff of programs serving women with problems such as homelessness, mental illness, or substance abuse may want to evaluate their program's effectiveness at meeting these needs as well as their effectiveness for women without such problems.

Sexual assault and domestic violence program staff are usually aware that certain program elements seem to be more effective than other program elements. For example, a sexual assault program's counseling staff may do very well helping women in counseling while also being aware that their response to emergency situations may be less helpful than they wish. Within advocacy services, their hospital response may, for any number of reasons, seem to work better than their court advocacy program. *Seem to work* is the important expression. Systematic evaluation may shed light on these disparate experiences. Evaluation may support their perceptions or provide evidence that their perceptions are not well founded. For example, evaluation may reveal that characteristics of "host staff" (physicians and nurses in hospitals, attorneys in courts) may affect outcomes. Medical staff may be more comfortable with the presence of an advocate than legal staff, for example. Such revelations are also possible without evaluation, but evaluation will often provide systematic data that can then be used to influence relevant decision makers.

Evaluation has a number of positive side effects. Agencies that embrace evaluation as a regular part of practice may be more likely to develop mechanisms to use evaluation results to enhance practice, more likely to support practitioners who systematically observe what they do, and more likely to create a climate in which staff look for alternate explanations for their observations. Evaluation has the potential to foster a climate of critical and constructive thinking that results in improved services, which in turn results in stronger evaluations.

The process of attempting an outcome evaluation may also have other positive side effects. In developing an evaluation strategy, evaluators typically will create a *logic model*, or flowchart, that links specific program elements to anticipated short- and long-term outcomes for participants. In developing these logic models, agencies may find that the goals and objectives that they intended their program to address are not targeted by specific program elements. In such cases, agencies may want to modify the program to specifically address those intended goals or may shift their thinking to adopt alternative, perhaps more realistic, goals for that program. Despite these positive features, not everyone sees evaluation as a positive experience for domestic violence and sexual assault programs.

RESISTANCE TO EVALUATION

Admittedly, the mutual reinforcement of evaluation and practice is not the way most staff will view evaluation, at least initially. At first, the link between evaluation and practice must usually be made by modeling. In a modeling situation, respected, experienced staff embrace evaluation, and newer, less experienced staff emulate what they see. Unfortunately, the opposite effect may also be modeled by experienced staff and administrators, when evaluation is seen as an unnecessary intrusion from the state, the funding source, or the board of directors. In such cases, evaluation may be viewed as a form of monitoring and surveillance.

Equating evaluation with surveillance is one of the primary reasons staff and agencies can be resistant to external requests or demands for program evaluation. This resistance has at its core a fear that funding for services will be reduced as a result of the evaluation. This is an understandable fear because the motivation for program evaluation by funding sources could be easily framed as one of surveillance. A more productive and positive way to frame program evaluation, acceptable to both funder and agency, is to view it as a tool for documenting both the amount and the quality of services provided. Ultimately, it may be that staff and agencies will use evaluation to improve their services and to better understand the effects that their interventions have on program participants, although it is clear that evaluation does not always have this effect.

Unfortunately, the need for information about effectiveness may seem to replicate for staff the same situation in which they find their clients: the victims of control by dominant others who have the power to exercise such control. Some staff may be unable or unwilling to verbalize these feelings of being controlled, particularly when the evaluation takes a traditional "top-down" approach. In a top-down approach, the funder or regulatory body usually dictates the process and content of the evaluation to the agency administration, who may in turn dictate the process and content of the evaluation to staff. Forcing staff to cooperate in an evaluation of their services in many ways replicates the abuses of power and control evident in domestic violence and sexual assault situations. In order to avoid replicating the abuse of power and control in an evaluation, agency staff must be included at the earliest possible stages when planning and developing the evaluation. Agency staff are experts concerning their services and the clients that they serve, and should be treated as such.

For a variety of other reasons, staff and administrators may be reluctant to undertake program evaluation. Practitioner resistance to evaluation usually has roots in lack of familiarity about the mechanics of evaluation and in resentment of the allocation of resources to something perceived as not helping sexual assault or domestic violence survivors. To expect practitioners to overcome their own reluctance to evaluate is a mistake akin to blaming the victim. If lack of familiarity and resources are, as we suggest, the sources of most resistance, then agencies, funders, and other relevant networks must bring about the conditions that adequately support the evaluation process.

The bottom line of program evaluation is accountability: to ourselves as workers, to our communities as taxpayers, and most important, to the victims about whose safety we worry. An agency that does not critically examine the effects of its interventions on those who it seeks to help is not an accountable agency. However, methods other than evaluation are available for an agency to be accountable to its clients and community. Such methods of maintaining accountability include conducting community focus groups to stay in touch with community needs, peer observation, providing quality supervision for both volunteer and paid staff, and establishing adequate client representation on governing boards. Some of these methods of accountability—focus groups, client input, and peer observation—are traditional elements of evaluation. In fact, the more an agency thinks seriously about being accountable, the closer it comes to meeting the conditions of evaluation.

QUESTIONABLE REASONS FOR EVALUATION

Edleson and his colleagues at the Domestic Abuse Project in Minneapolis identify motivations for evaluation that could lead to problems (Edleson & Frick, 1997). One of the most important uses of evaluation is as an aid to decision making. However, not all decisions are best made with evaluation data—some have to be made for political, economic, demand, funding, or staff training reasons. When evaluation data are used to make decisions more properly made using other considerations, a misuse of evaluation occurs. Decisions to alter or eliminate a program should not be shifted to the evaluator. Consider, for example, the domestic violence program administrator who is reluctant to apply for funding from the county mental health board because it would mean modifying the grassroots, feminist, empowerment-oriented agency with the entrapments of behavioral healthcare organizations, including diagnoses and treatment plans. Some staff may welcome the increasing professionalization demanded by the mental health funding whereas other staff may yearn for an agency driven by personal commitment, political belief, and shared values. Rather than take on the clash and overlap of these two equally valid perspectives, the agency may abdicate its decision making by bringing in an evaluator, hoping that evaluation may show the way out of a tough decision. Unfortunately in this situation, evaluation may not significantly inform the decision but only serve to delay it.

Every agency that undertakes evaluation envisions a positive result that can be used to support the agency in a variety of ways, usually funding and public image. However, when the primary motivation for evaluation is based in public relations and marketing, and no consideration has been made that the results might not be positive, such motivation may affect the evaluation methods or the dissemination of results if the results are not what agency authorities want them to be. It would be unusual in an evaluation to not find some negative results. In fact, negative evaluation results often lead to positive program changes. Agencies should discuss in advance how negative results will be used. A frank discussion about the possibility of negative results and what will be done with such results greatly reduces the chances that the evaluation will be shaped to produce only positive results, or that negative results will necessarily result in loss of funding.

A mundane but more important reason not to evaluate a program is a lack of resources, such as money, staff, and adequate support for evaluation. A poor evaluation will be of little use to anyone and may fuel sentiment that evaluation is a waste of time. Evaluation requires substantial money and time, and if either are underbudgeted, the evaluation will at best be of little use and at worst may be dangerous. If evaluation is added on by a funder or program administrator with no additional resources to conduct it, the evaluation is likely to fail.

ALTERNATIVE APPROACHES TO EVALUATION

In the traditional approach to evaluation, an outside evaluator performs the evaluation and reports to the funder and the agency. Underlying such an approach is the belief that an outside evaluator is capable of unbiased conceptualization, implementation, and interpretation. Staff are seen as biased toward positive findings, so their participation is often limited. Clients of the agency are viewed as the subjects of the outcome evaluation. Members of the client community or geographic community in which the evaluation occurs may be considered for comparison and demographic purposes.

During the past few decades, this traditional approach to evaluation has been augmented with alternative approaches that challenge the belief that objectivity is possible or even desirable. Such an approach often enhances the role of the client community in conceptualizing, implementing, and consuming evaluation. This alternate approach may be labeled *participatory evaluation* or an *empowerment approach.* Although these terms are often used interchangeably, they refer to slightly different approaches.

In participatory evaluation, agencies and evaluators work together to identify program processes and outcomes to be evaluated. The tools and protocols to be used in the evaluation are not imported by the evaluator as in the traditional approach but are selected and revised according to agency and client experience. Although not ignoring the value of providing evaluation data to funders and other third parties, the primary purpose of participatory evaluation is to provide agencies with information about program services to enable more informed decision making and problem solving.

Empowerment evaluation takes this a step further by using evaluation to foster organizational improvement and self-determination. Empowerment in this case refers to greater participation and control of the evaluation by agency staff, community, and clients. Empowerment also refers to enhancing the skills of the organization to conduct evaluation as well as improving the overall organizational process in a way deemed appropriate by the participants. An empowerment approach gives staff and community cooperative control over the development of the evaluation. Staff members, clients, and community members determine important procedures and outcomes, and conduct the evaluation with input and technical assistance from evaluators who are viewed as partners rather than controllers of evaluation. These evaluations can address program processes, outcomes, or both. The information can assist agencies in decision making and problem solving.

Traditional and alternate approaches to evaluation are not incompatible. The key difference between alternate and traditional approaches lies in the concept of power. In traditional approaches, evaluators are vested with power through knowledge, status, and credentials. In alternate approaches, these sources of power are divested to participants. The philosophies of domestic violence and sexual assault agencies are often quite compatible with the power sharing of alternate evaluation approaches. Consequently, domestic violence and sexual assault agencies are fertile ground for a hybrid of traditional and alternative approaches to evaluation.

In fact, the project that brought the authors of this text together was a hybrid approach. The funder's mandate, a traditional motive, brought the evaluation process into play. At the same time, the domestic violence and sexual assault communities in which the evaluation would occur had a tradition of participatory, empowerment-focused practices.

The evaluators had a foot in each of two worlds: rigorous research and community activism. Had the evaluators been traditional researchers, they would not have been acceptable to advocates; had they been activists only, they would have been unacceptable to the funder.

UNITS OF ANALYSIS: INDIVIDUAL, FAMILY, AND COMMUNITY

Programs may affect individuals, families, and communities. By individual effects, we mean changes in individuals who use the programs. Programs that target individual change are usually developed for perpetrators, victims, or significant others, such as programs designed for children who witness domestic violence or programs for partners of rape victims. Individual change targets may be cognitive (e.g., changes in attitudes or beliefs, improved decision making, changes in the belief that the assault or abuse was her fault), behavioral (e.g., renewing orders of protection, becoming more assertive, implementing a safety plan), or emotional (e.g., reduced anxiety, improved mood, increased feelings of safety). For the most part, programs and program goals in domestic violence and sexual assault agencies target individuals.

In other instances, the family may be the target of change. Instead of specifically attempting to change the behavior of individual family members, many family-oriented interventions attempt to change "family dynamics" or the way that family members interact with each other. This is distinct from changing the behaviors of individual family members. Outcomes of successful family interventions may include increased family cohesion and mutuality along with reduced conflict. Family goals are most common in counseling services for domestic violence and sexual assault victims and their children.

In addition to helping individual victims, perpetrators, family members, or families, however, much of what sexual assault and domestic violence agencies do is focused not on changing individuals or families but rather on changing larger systems, including the community response to violence. For example, advocating for mandatory arrest of batterers, helping to create a sexual assault task force, developing and supporting screening for domestic violence among emergency room patients, lobbying for changes in welfare reform to protect battered women, and increasing community awareness of the problems of sexual assault and domestic violence are legitimate activities of agencies. Several of these change targets may be outside the influence of a single agency (e.g., changes in welfare reform), but some community-level change targets may be the subject of evaluation (e.g., screening patients in emergency rooms for violence victims). Community-level evaluation is designed to capture the effects of programs at the community level. This is particularly appealing to agencies that deal with violence against women because such violence is believed to be maintained at a social, as well as an individual, level. Consequently, societal-level change is an appropriate target for evaluation, even for small societies such as communities and institutions. An excellent resource for these efforts is the *Evaluation Handbook for Community Mobilization: Evaluating Domestic Violence Activism* (Garske et al., 2000).

A related issue is accurately identifying the domain of an effect. Services designed for individual women should not be held accountable for outcomes outside their domain. Victim service agencies cannot expect to have an impact on offenders (other than through their community change component) because they do not deal directly with offenders. For example, battered women's advocates believe nothing a victim can do will change the behavior of her batterer; the batterer's change is within his domain, and in the domain of agencies whose job it is to influence him, such as batterer intervention programs, law enforcement, and the court. Consequently, reduction in the incidence of sexual assault and domestic violence is not an appropriate goal for victim service agencies, not because they don't want to see a reduction in violence but because the perpetrator's behavior is outside their sphere of direct influence (Sullivan, 1998). Although most victim service agencies understand that they cannot be held accountable for offender behavior, other community elements, funders, and even some program evaluators may not understand why this is so.

In this chapter, we have suggested that the primary reason for evaluation of domestic violence and sexual assault programs is accountability to consumers, to communities, and to the staff who provide the service. Used properly, evaluation helps us provide the best, safest services possible. Undertaking evaluation for reasons other than accountability (i.e., politics, marketing, or shifting the responsibility for decisions) is likely to lead to unsatisfactory results. Agencies may collect qualitative or quantitative data using traditional or nontraditional approaches. The approach and the way data are collected depend on the reasons for evaluation, the specific questions being asked, and the resources available. Although outcome evaluations commonly assess changes in knowledge, attitude, emotion, or action of individual clients, agencies can also look at changes in larger systems, including specific institutions or even community-wide responses to violence.

KEY POINTS

- The main reason to conduct an evaluation is accountability to our clients and our communities.
- Evaluation has the potential to foster a climate of critical and constructive thinking that results in improved services, which in turn results in stronger evaluations.
- Agency staff are experts concerning their services and the clients that they serve. Evaluation is less likely to succeed without staff input into the methods and procedures of the evaluation.
- Alternative approaches such as empowerment research and participatory evaluation complement the traditional approach to program evaluation.
- Outcome can be evaluated for community as well as individual units of change.

4

Basic Concepts in Evaluation

In this chapter, we will describe approaches evaluators use to answer questions about program implementation and effectiveness. This focus on the methodology of evaluation may be a review for some and wholly foreign to others, so we will aim for a middle ground when describing the components of evaluation that are applicable to domestic violence and sexual assault practitioners. The questions evaluation usually seeks to answer are as follows: (a) How do agencies provide services? and (b) What effect do the services have on program participants? The first question concerns the process of a program and the second question addresses the outcome of a program. Process and outcome evaluations are both important, so we will discuss each.

PROCESS EVALUATION

Process evaluation is used to describe or understand the important characteristics of a program, often with the aim of improving or replicating the program. Process evaluation tries to answer the questions "What kind of services are being provided to whom, how well, and how often?" Process data are also used to document program activities. Agencies often send reports to funders indicating the number of clients served, the type and number of hours of service provided, and the demographics of the clients served. All of this information could be considered process data.

Most domestic violence and sexual assault agencies use the basic elements of process evaluation without calling it that. Describing the characteristics of clients receiving services is one element of process. Counting the number of clients receiving services and the number of hours of service provided is another element of process. Evaluation formalizes these activities and provides a mechanism for using the information to alter services. For example, a domestic violence program located in a community where 45% of the residents are Hispanic may find that only 15% of their clients are Hispanic. Such an evaluation may suggest changes in staff, program, or ways of publicizing the program. Likewise, ongoing process evaluation may identify that the number of hours of direct service or the number of clients referred by the local hospital has declined. Staff may use these data in meetings or training with hospital staff, or in documenting a need for a liaison between the hospital and the agency.

The difference between conducting a process evaluation and simply collecting information is how the information is used. For example, an agency may routinely collect information on age, gender, ethnicity, and group attendance, reporting this information to funders or in an annual report. But does group attendance differ for clients of various ages and ethnicities? A process evaluation may be able to answer that and other questions, perhaps prompting staff to modify the program in a way that is more developmentally or culturally appropriate. Staff can then use the results of the process evaluation to guide discussion about how to increase group attendance among those who are underrepresented. In this example, the process evaluation enables staff to ask questions about attendance and also informs the discussion about what to do about it.

A special type of process evaluation is *needs assessment*, or collecting information to identify whether additional services are needed and whether staff have the skills to provide the needed services. Needs assessment often involves surveys and interviews of community residents, service providers, or community officials. Needs assessment may also use existing records such as census data, police records, and medical records. Getting information from a hospital about the proportion of emergency room visits in which women are injured during a sexual assault, for example, may be used to determine the need for a medical staff rape education program whereas tracking the number of domestic violence complaints at a police department or the number of protective orders issued by a court may support improvements in a coordinated community domestic violence prevention program.

Another special type of process evaluation is *evaluability assessment*. The knowledge gained from the assessment of how ready an agency or program is to conduct an evaluation can be one of the most beneficial aspects of the overall evaluation process. Evaluability assessments typically include determining whether program goals are linked to program activities, whether staff are properly trained for their roles, and whether program activities are being implemented consistently. Other key questions of evaluability focus on whether appropriate resources are in place to conduct the evaluation and whether the program is developed enough to make evaluation useful.

OUTCOME EVALUATION

In general, process evaluations focus on what programs do or need to do. At some point, however, we are interested in how people or systems change as a result of a program. This kind of evaluation is referred to as outcome evaluation. The task of outcome evaluation, as the name implies, is to determine the effectiveness of a program, or whether the program "works." The effect of a program for victims should be observable as a change in participants' knowledge, attitudes, beliefs, well-being, or behavior over time, or a change in system activity over time (such as the number of times that emergency room patients are screened for domestic violence).

The notion that a program's outcome is reflected in changes in individuals after receiving services is not without its critics. Some advocates believe that victims of crime do not need to change, so the outcome of programs that assist crime victims should not be looking for change in their clientele. Believing crime victims must change, this argument goes, is a form of blaming the victim or holding the victim in some way responsible, either for the crime or for preventing recurrence of the crime. Although this perspective is understandable, it reflects a limited notion of behavioral change and also confuses cause with response. Victims of tornadoes do not cause these storms nor are they responsible for preventing future storms. However, a program aiding victims of tornadoes probably wants to improve the victims' emotional and physical response to the tornado as well as increase the chances that both individuals and community systems will be better able to respond to victims of future tornadoes when they occur. Reducing the effects of injury and trauma, increasing coping skills, and adding knowledge of available resources are changes that can potentially be measured, whether the cause of the harm is a tornado, a batterer, or a rapist.

Process evaluation and outcome evaluation are complementary. In fact, outcome evaluation results are difficult to interpret without a full description of the services evaluated and the need for these services. Likewise, simply describing the services provided or the characteristics of people receiving services does not offer adequate information about the utility of a program. Process and outcome combine to provide a more complete picture of a program's usefulness.

INDICATORS OF PROCESS AND OUTCOME

Indicators of process or outcome are called data. Data are bits of information that are linked to the concepts, behaviors, or conditions that reflect how a program is delivered or the effect a program has on participants. Most people think of data as numbers and many kinds of data can be symbolized numerically: the number of counseling sessions attended, the number of minority clients served, a batterer's score on an attitude survey, or the number of times a survivor has called the crisis line. When indicators can be represented by numbers, we call them *quantitative* data. However, some indicators are better represented in other forms, such as words or pictures. These indicators are *qualitative* data. It is often assumed that outcome evaluation is going to be quantitative. In some cases, data in the form of numbers or graphs may better convey the information about the effects of a program, particularly if the consumers of the information are professionals or funders. In other cases, personal testimony from agency clients or pictures of resilient survivors may better convey the effects of a successful program. In most cases, both qualitative and quantitative data are collected for program evaluation and the choice about how to present these data is based on the purpose of the presentation and the intended audience.

Quantitative data are best used to indicate processes and outcomes that can easily be counted, such as arrests, group attendance, and statements with which participants can agree or disagree (on a scale of 1 to 10, for example). Standardized measures with predetermined response categories are a particular favorite of program evaluators, especially if the evaluation will gather information from a large number of people, or when a broad base of information is needed. Quantitative information is useful when the evaluation calls for systematic comparisons across people, programs, or organizations. Characteristics of a large number of clients can be summarized with quantitative data, making description an easier task.

Numerical information often reduces the variation and complexity of available data. Quantitative data analysis generally attempts to describe the "typical" experience of many, but not all, individuals in a sample. Using averages, for example, is one way in which complex data are simplified. Although this method is very convenient and efficient, the unique experiences of individuals in the sample will often be lost. The qualitative approach to data collection avoids stripping away too much information, overly reducing complex behavior to simple behavior, or trading meaning for ease of use. Qualitative data produce a richer, more detailed description of events. A qualitative evaluation approach might be used to provide a greater depth of information. The story of a rape survivor, for example, and how an agency's services helped her following the assault, may have more meaning to some audiences than an average score on a scale measuring reduction in rape trauma for all clients from a given agency. Of course, in order to provide such rich descriptions, qualitative evaluation usually focuses on fewer people. In general, qualitative program evaluation is quite labor intensive.

COLLECTING DATA

Empirical evaluation refers to the use of information that is available through observation or experience. Evaluators often prefer numbers because they are a shorthand way of recording observations and experiences, but writing down an exact quote from a client also forms an empirical record. Evaluators have four ways of collecting information: observing, interviewing, using paper-and-pencil forms like tests and surveys, and using existing records.

Observation. One way of collecting evaluation information is to observe what people and programs do. By observation, we mean not only watching them but also listening to what they say. Counselors often systematically observe how clients behave, such as watching how they interact in a shelter or what they say in a counseling session or during a crisis call. These observations can be documented to form a valid record that can be used to document client progress. We can also observe clients formally, such as counting the number of times they speak during a community meeting or documenting their interaction with their children. In batterer intervention programs, staff may listen for the use of terms like "the old lady" or "the little woman" and use this information to judge a man's progress in the program. Victim service agencies may listen for language that reflects a client's belief that she can do what needs to be done to stay safe or improve her life. For example, an advocate may listen for a battered

woman's description of implementing a safety plan. Observation is an
undervalued method of collecting data for quantitative program evaluation but is a standard method of collecting qualitative data. For
example, quantitative observation is more likely to have a specified
observational checklist with specific things to tally whereas qualitative
observation is more likely to use the observer's field notes written in
a narrative form, including interpretations.

Interviews. In evaluation language, conducting a formal conversation
with clients for the purpose of collecting data is called an *interview*
and this is an important method for gathering evaluation information.
Interviews are often structured, such as asking a victim a series of predetermined questions about the frequency and severity of her abuse.
Interview questions may be open ended (e.g., "Tell me about the
abuse") or closed ended (e.g., "How many times have you been physically abused in the last 30 days"). Quantitative approaches to data
collection usually prefer closed-ended questions whereas qualitative
approaches favor open-ended questions. In fact, qualitative evaluators
may avoid questions entirely in favor of conversations, in which a
concerted effort is made to avoid structuring the client's response.
Quantitative approaches are more likely to provide response categories to interview questions.

Sexual assault, medical, and law enforcement staff may conduct
formal interviews with rape survivors dictated by the needs of evidence collection. Batterers may be formally interviewed to evaluate
their perceived level of responsibility for their abuse, their motivation
for change, and current lethality. Interviews with battered women
may be unstructured, usually beginning with a question or request,
such as asking that she talk about her use of a safety plan. Whether
interviews are structured or unstructured, responses to formal and
informal interviews can be documented and coded, forming a source
of data for program evaluation.

Paper-and-pencil approaches. Staff may be used to thinking of evaluation as written surveys, either one-time-only questionnaires or measures given before and after an intervention. In fact, paper-and-pencil
approaches to data collection are common in evaluation. The advantage
of paper-and-pencil measures is ease of use in the data collection and
analysis process. Staff can give an entire group of clients, such as
shelter residents, a questionnaire to complete at a given time. Because
questionnaires can often be self-administered, they have the potential to
be administered anonymously, unlike interviews or direct observation.
Participants usually respond to preexisting categories that generally do

not require additional coding. Written questionnaires do not usually involve documenting quotes or other observations and because they are already structured, they make efficient use of time and other evaluation resources. Standardized scales and indices are favored by researchers because they have previously described characteristics of accuracy (validity) and consistency (reliability) important to evaluators. Not surprisingly, paper-and-pencil measures are sometimes overused because of their facility. The drawback to paper-and-pencil approaches, particularly those involving fixed responses and standardized tests, is that program participants are limited in what kind of information they can provide. In addition, standardized paper-and-pencil measures might not be appropriate with all types of clients, such as the young, the old, gays or lesbians, and clients who have limited literacy.

Existing records. Some data collected for other purposes may be appropriate for use in evaluation. In particular, emergency room records, police reports, and court data are potentially useful to sexual assault and domestic violence programs, but these data are probably the most underused, particularly for victim service agencies. Needs assessment often depends on an analysis of existing data from criminal justice, social service, and medical records collected for other reasons. Likewise, existing information about program activities, processes, decisions, and other background data can be very useful. Such data can be used as a guide to develop interview questions and observational procedures in outcome evaluation.

RELIABILITY AND VALIDITY

Regardless of how evaluation data are collected (observation, interview, paper and pencil, or use of existing records), the reliability and validity of the data are a primary concern. The main characteristic of a reliable measure is its ability to detect a condition when the condition is present. For example, a reliable measure of social support will indicate a certain level of support before the intervention, and if the amount of social support in a woman's life increases during her involvement in the program, the measure will indicate a numerical increase in social support after the program. Each form of data collection has its own threats to reliability. A problem with the use of existing records is that evaluators may not know how consistently the records were kept. If using arrest records as the main indicator of need or as an outcome for a domestic violence program, for example, we must be aware that arrest does not reliably measure the incidence of domestic abuse in a community. For example, Dutton and his colleagues (1997) found that the proportion of arrest to victim-reported abuse was 1 in 35; that is, for every reported arrest, there were 35 assaultive actions. For observations and interviews, *interrater reliability* is a primary concern. The question here is whether two different people using the same interview with the same client would get similar answers to the interview questions. For paper-and-pencil methods, an assessment tool is considered reliable if a person's answers to the questions do not change significantly due to *extraneous variables*. Extraneous variables can be anything other than the construct that the survey is intended to measure that affects a person's responses to the survey, such as the time of day that the survey was administered, whether it was administered by a male or female, the mood of the person answering the questions, and so on. In order to maximize the reliability of a data collection method, the setting, time, people collecting the data, and data collection procedures should remain consistent throughout the period of data collection if at all possible.

The validity of a data collection method, or the ability of a measure to accurately detect what it purports to measure, is another concern that is related to, but separate from, the reliability of a measure. Clearly, a measure that is not reliable cannot be valid. For a simple example, consider measuring a person's weight using an old bathroom scale. Imagine that depending on how gently a person steps onto the scale, the reading might vary by as much as 30 pounds. Obviously, this scale would not be a valid measure for the success of a weight loss program because of the scale's unreliability. On the other hand, just because a measure is reliable doesn't mean that it is valid for our particular use. Although we can measure a person's weight very consistently from day to day and in a variety of settings using an accurate digital scale, using a person's weight to predict the likelihood that they will engage in violence is not a *valid* use of that measure. For a more relevant example, if reduced scores on a "violence supportive attitudes" measure are used as an indicator of the success of a high school based prevention program, yet 50% of the participants who score low on that measure go on to engage in violence in their relationships, then that measure is not a valid measure of the program's success, regardless of how reliably it can measure a person's attitudes. As suggested here, validity does not exist in the measure itself, but rather in how the measure is used.

Multiple methods. In general, the best evaluations adopt multiple methods of data collection. To the extent possible, agencies should collect both quantitative and qualitative information. A combination of interviews, questionnaires, observation, and use of existing records makes a much stronger evaluation than using any one method alone. Within any form of data collection, it is advisable to provide opportunities for different responses. For example, a closed-ended survey should include a section in which open-ended responses are also solicited. Using multiple methods and including an option for open-ended responses in which participants may explain or qualify their answer will increase the probability that valid and reliable data will be obtained.

OUTCOME EVALUATION DESIGN

Many factors can influence behavioral or systematic change and the program will be only one of those factors. The accuracy of an evaluation in attributing observable change to a program or service rather than to the numerous other factors that may influence change is determined by the design of the evaluation. For example, a woman's agency may offer a 12-week education and support group for survivors of sexual assault and evaluate the outcome of this program using a measure of rape trauma syndrome as an indicator. In addition to the program, however, other factors will influence the score on a measure of rape trauma syndrome, including the prerape psychological state of the survivor, the severity of the assault, support from her family, substance abuse, and her relationship to the offender.

In general, the stronger the evaluation design, the more confidence we have in a program's ability to take credit for any measured change in clients. The primary questions to consider in evaluation design are as follows: (a) How many times will clients be evaluated? and (b) Will there be a comparison group? Strong designs feature at least two points of measurement and at least one comparison group. However, evaluation design decisions are usually based on practical considerations such as the amount of time involved, availability of resources, and availability of appropriate comparison groups. Above all, it is important to ask how much information is necessary to answer the questions that must be answered by a program evaluation. For example, it may not be necessary to rule out other causes of change when the funding source is interested only in whether clients change. For most practitioners, it is important only that their clients get better or safer and it is not necessary to account for exactly what caused the change. However, when developing programs to replicate or market to others, it may be more important to know exactly which components work and whether any unintended effects occur.

Single-group designs. This simplest of evaluation designs gathers information about whether clients have mastered a task, such as developing a safety plan or understanding the characteristics of an abusive relationship. If one objective of your program is that participants will be able to identify three characteristics of an abusive relationship and, after your program, 90% of the participants are able to identify three characteristics of an abusive relationship, then you have at least some evidence of your program's success. One problem with this design is that services for victims of domestic violence and sexual assault are usually not trying to teach specific material but rather are trying to change a wide range of attitudes, beliefs, skills, and knowledge, and the aim is often to move people along in the right direction rather than getting them to achieve some level of mastery. Another problem with this evaluation design arises when someone asks the question, "How would the participants have performed if they hadn't had your program?" To answer this question, a prepost design or a no-treatment control group design would be necessary.

The single group design can be strengthened by adding a measurement prior to the program, or a "pretest." The posttest is compared to the pretest and any difference *might be* attributable to the program. When little time exists between the premeasure and the postmeasure, you can be more confident that the changes in participants' scores are a result of your program. However, if the program spans several weeks, one might argue that other life experiences might be responsible for the change in scores rather than your intervention.

Comparison group designs. Another way to strengthen the argument that your program was responsible for positive findings is to administer the evaluation instrument to a group of people who are not in your program, called a comparison group. One type of comparison group is a "no-treatment control group" that is made up of individuals who get no program or intervention. By using a no-treatment control group, we are able to demonstrate how, after participation in our program, people differ from a similar group who did not receive the intervention. Although waiting lists are not common in many sexual assault and domestic violence agencies, a waiting list is the most ethical source of a no-treatment control group, both because it is a naturally occurring control rather than one created for research and because the people on the waiting list will eventually get the intervention. An alternative kind of comparison group is a group receiving a different program or a different kind of intervention for the same issue. By providing two interventions, you avoid the practical and ethical problem of not providing services to a group of participants. Here, the difficulty is finding a group of people that *do not* differ significantly on important characteristics from the people that participated in your program and finding an alternate intervention that *does* differ significantly from the program you wish to evaluate.

Regardless of whether the comparison group gets no intervention or an alternate intervention, there may be substantial preexisting differences between the participants in the two groups. One way to increase the likelihood that the two groups are as similar as possible is to randomly assign individuals to the intervention group and to the control group. In this way, any preexisting factors that might influence the outcome measure should be equally distributed between the two groups. Random assignment is difficult to implement, however, and is usually beyond the scope of sexual assault and domestic violence program evaluation. As an alternative to random assignment, evaluators can examine the differences between the two groups and use statistical techniques to control for those differences.

Client satisfaction. In light of the design difficulties in evaluating outcomes, some agencies turn to less complex indicators of success, such as measuring how program participants feel about the services they received or how satisfied they are with these services (Sullivan, 1998). Typical satisfaction questions include "What did you like/dislike about the program? Would you recommend this program to a friend? How helpful was this program?" Results of satisfaction surveys give us an indication of how well our program was received, suggest aspects of the program that might be modified or expanded, and let us know whether the program is perceived as being helpful. Often, the results of satisfaction surveys are quite positive, so they can be a useful tool in increasing service providers' morale and preventing caregiver fatigue. The shift to managed health care in the United States has made client satisfaction a priority because a satisfied client is more likely to use services than an unsatisfied client. However, client satisfaction must not be confused with outcome evaluation. The outcome of a program indicates how participants change as a result of the program, not whether they are satisfied with the program. Client satisfaction is a judgment on the delivery of services (i.e., process), not a judgment about their own change as a result of the services. In an experiment by Schewe and O'Donohue (1993), two independent rape prevention programs were presented to different groups of students. Although both programs received equally high marks on a satisfaction survey covering the credibility and helpfulness of the program, one of the programs was not at all effective in achieving desirable outcomes whereas the other program was moderately effective in producing desired changes among program participants. If only the satisfaction survey was used in this study, both programs would have appeared equally "effective." Use of an outcome evaluation, however, revealed that students in one of the programs demonstrated positive changes in knowledge, attitudes, and behavioral intentions whereas students in the other group evidenced almost no change.

In summary, a wide variety of approaches to evaluation is available to agencies and which approach is selected will depend on the nature of the questions to be addressed by the evaluation, the level of confidence needed in the results, and the resources available for supporting the evaluation. Random assignment to treatment groups is usually not necessary to answer questions about program effectiveness asked by funders, boards of directors, and staff. Nor would such an experiment, even if desirable, be possible under the conditions of practice in most agencies and communities. However, the questions now being asked of domestic violence and sexual assault agencies usually require responses beyond those of merely counting the types and number of hours of service provided or documenting client satisfaction with those services. In this chapter, we presented varying approaches to data collection and evaluation design to assist agencies that need to conduct evaluations of their services. The challenge to us all is to balance the kind of information requested and the level of confidence required of our results with the resources we have available.

KEY POINTS

- The basic questions of evaluation are as follows: (a) Are we providing the service that we intended to provide? and (b) What effect does this service have on program participants? Answers to the first question are reached through *process evaluation* and answers to the second question are reached through *outcome evaluation.*
- Quantitative data are best used to indicate processes and outcomes that can easily be counted or when the evaluation calls for systematic comparisons across people, programs, or organizations.
- Qualitative data are best used to understand in-depth, detailed information, often in participants' own words.
- There are four ways of collecting data: observing, interviewing, using paper-and-pencil tests, or using existing records.
- The *reliability* or consistency of a measure and the *validity* or accuracy of a measure depend not only on the measure but also on how they are used in evaluation.
- The primary questions to consider in evaluation design are as follows: (a) How many times will clients be evaluated? and (b) Will there be a comparison group?

5

Using Evaluation Results

Perhaps the most important aspect of conducting an evaluation is using the results. This chapter will describe several ways that you may use the results once you have completed an outcome evaluation. First we discuss how to use evaluation results to improve services and then we consider how to communicate the results to various audiences: service delivery staff, boards of directors and other stakeholders, the community and potential clients, and current or potential funding agencies.

HOW TO USE EVALUATION RESULTS
TO IMPROVE SERVICES

The results of an evaluation typically produce mixed emotions. Invariably, not all of the results will turn out as expected. Although some of the results will be validating and rewarding, others will be disappointing. Because most agencies believe that the services they offer have positive outcomes for clients, negative outcomes are often discouraging, suggesting ways in which your services were not help-ful. Nevertheless, these unexpected outcomes may provide the most information about your services and how to improve them. It is important not to equate disappointing results with failure. If the results of your evaluation are negative, then at least you have become aware of your program's shortcomings. Once an area of weakness is identified, however, the next step is to begin the sometimes arduous task of modifying the service or program. The next section discusses ways to make use of these unexpected results, while later we discuss ways to communicate the results of your evaluation to others.

Unexpected Outcomes

Any evaluation will likely reveal some negative aspects of a program. The important thing is to determine how best to use these data to improve your program. Sometimes, your evaluation will present you with knowledge you are glad to learn. For example, process data may reveal that you are not serving the same demographic groups you earlier believed you were serving. If you learn that your agency serves mostly women below the age of 18, when previously you believed that you were serving women from the ages of 17 to 25, that information can be used to improve your staff training or outreach services.

Other times, the unexpected outcomes of your evaluation will be disappointing. For instance, you may learn that your counseling program's intention to improve clients' self-efficacy resulted in no change in clients' confidence in their ability to solve their daily problems. In this situation, the evaluation results can be used several ways to improve your program. First, meet with your counselors to discuss the results of this evaluation. (See also the section on "Tailoring Your Report to Your Audience" and specifically "Reports to Service Providers and Program Directors.") Focus your discussion on two points:

Is this information accurate? For example, is self-efficacy really not changing as a result of counseling or is there some problem with the way that "self-efficacy" is measured that is responsible for the results? Is it possible that as victims of violence begin to address their trauma in therapy, it causes them to respond to the outcome measure in an unexpected way? Or is there some other problem with the measure that is responsible for the finding of no change? Alternatively, some constructs (such as self-efficacy) may not be likely to change as the result of a short-term intervention. Evaluation measures may need to be rewritten so that they are more sensitive to relatively small changes in beliefs or behaviors or the length of time between pre- and post-intervention assessments may need to be lengthened.

Is there something about the intervention that is causing it to be ineffective and, if so, what can be done to improve the intervention? Questions to consider in this discussion include: Why are counseled clients not showing an increase in self-efficacy? How can we change the way we work with clients to help increase their sense of self-efficacy? Are other programs, curricula, or strategies available that have proven to be effective for increasing self-efficacy? Can we get more input from clients on how to improve the intervention? Should we ask an external supervisor or consultant for her or his input into this matter? Instead of getting discouraged by unexpected outcomes, explore the most accurate interpretation of the results and the best ways to achieve the desired outcomes.

Meeting Unmet Needs

Often, your evaluation will provide you with additional information about your clients' unmet needs and how to address those needs. You may learn that your clients would like more counseling services or a 24-hour hotline. Modifying the manner in which services are delivered to better meet clients' needs is a possible outcome of evaluation results.

One advantage of conducting a careful evaluation is that it will identify which parts of your program work and for whom. When focusing on program improvement, you can model the weaker aspects of your program after ones you find to be most effective. For example, if you find you are having greater success with older women than younger women who call your hotline, you can use that information in any one of a number of ways. You might use the process evaluation data you have collected to determine which aspects of your hotline were not effective with younger women. If the process data you have collected directly address this issue, you can determine why those aspects of your program were not as useful to them and alter those aspects of your program.

Often, however, evaluation results can inform you of a problem without explaining it sufficiently to be fixed. For example, your evaluation data may inform you that there is a weakness in your hotline and indicate among whom, but does not detail the specific problem. In this case, you could interview clients and ask them how to improve the services (recognizing that you will not be able to make all of their suggestions a reality) or meet with staff who run the hotline to brainstorm possible improvements.

HOW TO COMMUNICATE THE RESULTS
OF YOUR EVALUATION

After completing an evaluation, it is likely that you will want to present your data to at least one of these audiences: (a) stakeholders and funders, for the purpose of generating additional support for your programs; (b) service providers and program administrators, for the purpose of modifying and improving services; and (c) the community, for the purpose of improving public relations and generating public support for your programs.

For any given service, agencies typically report how many people the agency serves, the types of needs clients generally have, the direct benefits clients receive, and any gains in skills, knowledge, attitudes, behavior, or health and well-being that result from your agency's services. The information that is presented, as well as the way that it is presented, will vary depending on the audience and the purpose of the presentation. For example, if you are reporting to the community, you will probably want to avoid statistical or evaluative jargon as much as possible. In this case, replacing complex discussion of your data analyses with a simple report of frequencies and percentages, and replacing terms like process and outcome with a report of your methods, will help you avoid alienating your audience. Likewise, a brochure designed to raise awareness or a report to funders may have certain information that must be included or formats to be followed. However, regardless of your target audience, there is some information that most everyone (potential clients, funders, community members, and other stakeholders) will want to know. This includes information about your services and your clients as well as information gained from your evaluation. The following sections describe information typically included in most evaluation reports; we will distinguish between audiences later in this chapter.

Program Description

Information about your service. Whatever the format, typically a report includes information about your agency and the services you provide. This section will consist largely of information you had prior to the evaluation. Start with the basics: Who are you and where are you located? How can people contact you? Do clients need an appointment or do you have walk-in services? How can people get to your office? Can you go to your clients instead? What types of services do you provide? To whom? Who is your staff? How extensively has your staff been trained? By whom has your staff been trained? What collaborations do you have in place to provide additional services and referrals to your clients? Many potential clients who approach a community agency may be wary; providing information about your agency and the services it provides may help alleviate the tension.

Information about your clients. Most audiences will want to know some information about whom your program serves. First, you could indicate how many people come to your agency during a given time. Then, you may want to describe the characteristics of both your typical client and the range of clients whom you serve. Provide enough detail about each so that someone who is unfamiliar with your community can get a sense of whom it is you serve. Client and community demographics that you may want to report include age, race, marital status, primary language, socioeconomic status, and area of residence (e.g., rural, urban). Depending on your audience and the type of services you offer, you also may want to include information on the gender or sexual orientation of your clients. Other characteristics might include the primary presenting problems of your clients, additional problems and barriers to health commonly experienced by clients and community residents, and client and community strengths.

Next, consider your clients' unmet needs. Are there barriers or a lack of resources that prevent clients from accessing your services? Is homelessness, illiteracy, or a lack of adequate health care a problem in your community? Are there problems with transportation, child care, or language that make it difficult for some residents to access your agency's services? Supplying this information will help you petition for funding later, will give a more complete description of your clientele, and will highlight the importance of the services that you provide. For example, if you discover that more and more of the people coming to your agency speak only Spanish but your agency only has one staff person proficient in Spanish, you may be able to use this information to justify a request for funding for another bilingual staff person. For structured programs (i.e., ones with a beginning and end point) as opposed to walk-in services (which may not have a particular end point), you may want to report how many people complete the program compared to how many people start the program. For those who drop out, why haven't they seen it through? Ideas about what may be done to alleviate those barriers could also be included in this section.

Information Gained from the Evaluation

Your questionnaires. Once information about your clients and services has been provided, you may want to include information gained from the evaluation itself. Although the detail regarding data analysis and results will vary based on your audience, you will generally start with the evaluation procedures: What data were collected, how often, and from whom. It may be useful to state why you chose your method of data collection.

> We began the Client Satisfaction Evaluation with our hotline. Once a week, for 24 hours at a time, we collected data from every client who placed a call. In order to avoid sampling bias, we rotated the data collection days so that every week, we collected data on a different day.

Include a thorough description of your measures, whether they be questionnaires, surveys, or interviews. For example, you could state that your questionnaires were multiple choice and asked about how helpful your agency's hotline services were. Giving that information along with your results will make it clear to your readers what your questions were like.

> Eighty-five percent of callers stated that our hotline gave them a lot more information than they had prior to their call, 12% stated our hotline gave them somewhat more information, and only 3% stated that our hotline gave them little more information than they had prior to their call.

Notice that the above description provides useful data about the program as well as a listing of the response choices from the evaluation measure. Often, complex questionnaires (e.g., with different formats, response choices) require a lot of description in order for an outside reader to get a clear idea of your questionnaire or interview. Including a copy of your measures in an appendix to your report may allow you to shorten your description in the text.

The benefits of your program. Next, you may want to discuss whatever benefits you have discovered as a result of the evaluation. If you have data from before your clients came to your agency and data from after they have received services, describe how they improved. Below are two examples of how to present before-and-after data. The first is an example of a case-by-case qualitative report. The second is an example of a quantitative report.

> Report 1: One client who filled out the qualitative portion of our interview stated in her "before" interview: "I hope the counselors at this agency know how to treat people. I have been treated like a child at other agencies and I'm not going to put up with it here." In a later survey, she stated, "Thank you for trying to help me without acting like I'm some little kid."

> Report 2: At their intake interviews, clients indicated that a number of positive self-statements (i.e., statements regarding their level of perceived support, problem-solving and decision-making abilities, level of self-control and self-efficacy, ability to talk about the abuse) were, on average, "sometimes" true for them. When

surveyed an average of eight sessions later, these same clients indicated that the positive self-statements were "often" true for them.

Once such statements have been made, you may wish to add to them by including data about one particular client.

For example, one woman who sought help at our agency went from scoring a 68% on Time Management Skills to scoring an 82%. This degree of improvement was typical of our clients.

However, obtaining before-and-after data is often difficult and many agencies do not have the resources to collect it. What you may have instead is data collected from the clients describing how the clients feel now that they have spent time with the staff at your agency. This type of data collection ("post only" or "after only"; see Chapter 4) will still provide you with ample results to include in your evaluation report. This type of data collection is most useful if you are interested in how helpful clients found your staff and services rather than measuring how much your clients changed.

Tailoring Your Report to Your Audience

Reports to funders. Funders often indicate what they would like to see in reports. If they do not, then tell them as much as possible, focusing on the results of your evaluation. In some cases, your funders have designed your evaluation measures. Hence, they may know exactly what data you have collected over the evaluation period. For cases in which funders are not familiar with the evaluation design and measures, you may want to discuss with them the content of the measures to determine what they would like to see in reports.

Reports to service providers and program directors. Presenting evaluation results to agency staff may involve written reports, face-to-face presentations, and work groups. For this audience, you need to provide the details of the measurement tools and the results. If you have before-and-after data on clients, service providers need to know exactly how and in what way participants improved and perhaps, more important, in what way they did not improve. You may want to discuss who (e.g., age, ethnicity, gender, education, income, family make-up, types of presenting problems) improved and who did not improve and consider reasons for these differences. The best methods for improving services will come from an in-depth consideration of what the results mean. In some instances, discussion may reveal that

Table 5.1   Tailoring Your Report to Your Audience

Audience	Types of Presentations	Content	Level of Detail Regarding Services Offered	Typical Level of Detail from the Evaluation
Funders	Written reports, site visits, oral presentations	Describe services and evaluation efforts, but focus on the results.	Medium: Remind them of details, but remember they are familiar with you as a recipient of funds.	High: But not necessarily complex.
Community	Brochures, web page, press release, oral presentations	Describe services & positive impacts. Use narrative with numbers only to emphasize points.	High: This will be the first time that many people hear or learn about your services.	Low
Service Providers & Program Directors	Written reports, face-to-face presentations, work groups	Interactive discussion of how evaluation results can be used to improve services.	Low: These people already know the services.	High: For both process and outcome evaluation.

the measurement tool was flawed or did not capture the constructs that the program intended to change. In other cases, you will learn that the program needs to accommodate different populations, emphasize different constructs (e.g., skills, knowledge, attitudes, behavior), or modify other aspects of service delivery (e.g., time, location, language).

Reports to the community. Sharing the results of your evaluation with the community (and hence, with potential clients) may be done through brochures, Web pages, or press releases. This type of report, therefore, will need a touch of marketing as you consider who the members of your community are. Here you will want to tell a story using more narrative and present numbers only to highlight important

Table 5.2

As a result of this phone call, how much more information, if any, do you have about the choices available to you?	#	%
A lot more	2000	40
Somewhat more	1000	20
A little more	250	5
No more	75	1.5
Missing/don't know	1675	33.5
Total	5000	100

points. Participant statements and testimonials, used with their permission, are an effective way to make a point. Report a few attention-getting facts about your agency and the effectiveness of your services. Use charts, tables, graphs, pictures, and bulleted lists to make the information easy to read and understand. Explanations geared to community members about programs should be simple and direct. Avoid jargon and avoid a lot of the detail that funders and service providers want to know. Table 5.1 highlights some of these details.

Presentation of Your Evaluation Reports

Written reports, brochures, press releases, and face-to-face presentations are common methods for sharing evaluation results. When choosing form and content, use the results of your evaluation to support the story that you want to tell. Supplement the data and numbers that you present with testimonials and statements from participants. Funders may also want to see the ratio of program effects to program cost (e.g., the cost per unit of change). Such cost-effect analysis may be more useful to funders and agency administrators than to practitioners or community constituents.

Visual representations of your results. When you have a lot of data to present to your audience, nontext representations such as tables often work best. A table or a graph can depict a lot of data quickly and clearly. A word of caution: If you can break down or simplify a table, do it. Large tables may be intimidating and difficult to read. Fortunately, most word processing programs today provide easy formatting. Below we give examples of tables with varying levels of detail.

When the most important thing is clarity, try the example in Table 5.2.

Table 5.3

In what language was the survey administered?	#	%
English	68	98.6%
Spanish	1	1.4%
Total	69	100%

Table 5.4

Service	Your Agency	All Agencies Nationwide
Additional crisis lines	10%	5%
Attorney	10%	10%
911 or police	5%	5%
Community education	1%	5%
Counseling	30%	20%
Criminal justice advocate	3%	10%
Employment services	1%	3.0%
Financial assistance	5%	2%
Housing services	0%	5%
Services for children	10%	10%
Services for offenders	5%	2%
Shelter	10%	1%
Substance abuse services	5%	5%
Disease or pregnancy testing	0%	5%
Other	10%	10%

If there isn't too much information, you may be able to omit gridlines, as shown in Table 5.3.

With a lot of rows (or columns), it is helpful to provide shading, as you can see in Table 5.4.

Notice that in addition to providing shading or gridlines in the tables, changing the font size or making some headings bold, capitalized, or italicized can also clarify the data you are presenting.

Depending on your data, you may be able to use other graphics in addition to or instead of tables. The type of graphic will depend, of course, on what type of data you want to display. If you have categorical or nominal data, that is, data that involve categories or groups of people, you may want to use a bar graph or pie chart (see Figure 5.1).

Figure 5.1 What language did your caller speak?

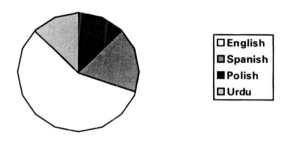

Figure 5.2   What language did your caller speak?

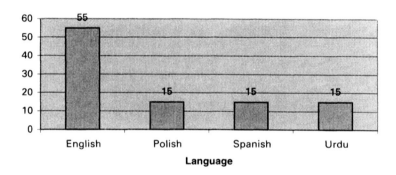

Categorical data, as shown by Figure 5.2, can also be displayed well in bar charts.

If you cannot label the bars, you may want to make them different colors or patterns and include a key. If you are working in a situation in which visibility is a problem, it may be a good idea to avoid 3-D effects. If you are trying to show improvement in your clients over time, you might try a different type of graphic. Ideally, different colors should be used, but if you are working in black and white, you can help your reader keep track of which line represents which group by using other means, like pattern and thickness of lines (see Figure 5.3).

Oral Presentations

How you present the data is sometimes as important as what you present. Your manner of presentation will affect how your audience

Figure 5.3   Number of Hotline Calls by Area of City

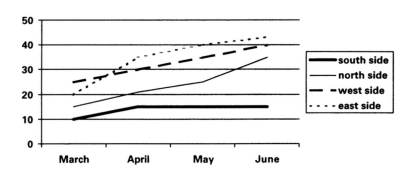

receives your material. Here are several points to keep in mind as you prepare an oral presentation of your evaluation results.

- Make your presentation flow like a story.
- Have a few key points and make sure what you say supports those points.
- Be organized—avoid rummaging around with multiple sheets of paper.
- Avoid reading to your audience.
- Don't go overtime. If your talk is scheduled for 15 minutes, make sure you only prepare 15 minutes of information (i.e., limit yourself to three or four main points).

Visual aids. Visual aids are often an important aspect of oral presentations. However, they need to fit well into your talk. That is, they need to contribute to, rather than distract from, what you are saying. When using overheads, follow some basic guidelines.

- Keep your typeface (font) size large (around a 20-point font on a computer). Your overheads need to be easy to read.
- When choosing typeface, a new or unusual font can lighten up the presentation, but make sure to consider a couple of things: (a) Will a cute font threaten your credibility or professionalism? (b) Are your fonts hard to read? You may need to bold or enlarge the text to make sure your overhead is legible.
- Do not go too fast; allow two minutes for each overhead. If you give a 10-minute presentation, you can include three to five overheads.
- Although transparencies are expensive, don't try to cram everything onto as few as possible. Try to limit yourself to one main idea per transparency. Also, don't be afraid of skipping lines and indenting for visual clarity. An overhead cluttered with text is difficult to read and may be confusing.

- Using bullet points or an outline form in your overhead can serve the dual purpose of keeping your audience with you *and* keeping you aware of where you are in your talk. Also, this may help you remember to keep only the basic points on the overhead because you will be elaborating on these with your verbal presentation.
- Using colors, borders, and backgrounds can add a finished look to your overheads, but take care to avoid using dark backgrounds, which may limit visibility. As much as possible, go for simple designs that will not distract viewers from the content of your talk.
- Try not to block the screen when giving a presentation. This is sometimes easy to forget because you often need to stand directly in front of a projector in order to write on or change transparencies.
- Cover up points on the overhead you have not gotten to yet. This is less for the value of suspense than it is to keep your audience from reading ahead and, hence, losing track of what you are presenting.

SUMMARY

Conducting an outcome evaluation is not simply a discrete event, but part of an ongoing process. More and more, we hear legislators and policy-makers refer to "outcome-based practice." As the phrase implies, outcome evaluation becomes an integral part of service provision, guiding not only the agency's policies and services, but also individual practice.

The cycle of evaluation may begin with a funder mandate;
that leads to the creation of logic models;
that leads to the creation of outcome measures and evaluation procedures;
that guides the collection and analysis of data;
that needs to be interpreted against the context of your agency, your staff, your clients, and your community;
that is reported back to funders, staff, and the community;
and ultimately is used to improve the services and to modify the outcome measures and evaluation procedures.

With an improved understanding of the strengths and weaknesses of the services, and with improved outcome measures and procedures, the cycle of evaluation may then be repeated.

KEY POINTS

- The most important part of conducting an evaluation project is using the results of that project to meet the original purpose of the evaluation.

- Evaluation data can be used both to improve services and to document the effectiveness of those services.
- Evaluation reports need to be tailored to the needs of specific audiences such as (a) stakeholders and funders, for the purpose of generating additional support; (b) service providers and program administrators, for the purpose of modifying and improving services; and (c) the community, for the purpose of improving public relations and generating public support for your programs.

PART III:
Lessons Learned

6

Lessons Learned in Evaluating Domestic Violence and Sexual Assault Services

As emphasized throughout other chapters in this book, evaluating domestic violence and sexual assault services presents numerous ethical, philosophical, and methodological challenges. This book emerged from an evaluation of domestic violence and sexual assault services in Illinois, and this chapter will provide lessons learned from our experience as a case study to understand evaluation challenges in the context of a real example. Although programs in other places may not be identical to those in Illinois, the issues we raise here are generalizable to many situations. We worked collaboratively with programs across the state to develop and implement an outcome evaluation of services for women who have experienced rape or domestic violence. Some of the issues addressed here are specific to the four service components that we evaluated (i.e., hotline, advocacy, counseling, and shelter); other concerns are general to evaluating services for survivors of violence. Appendixes A and B contain the measures we developed. Statistical information about specific items and indices, as well as other information about this project, may be found on our Web site at www.uic.edu/depts/psch/idhs.

In May 1998, the Illinois Department of Human Services initiated an evaluation of all state-funded domestic violence and sexual assault services in Illinois. The first statewide evaluation of such services in the United States, this pioneering effort involved 87 programs in data collection during 1999 and 2000. More than 26,000 evaluation forms were completed by agency clients, measuring outcomes of the following services: crisis hotline, brief and extended advocacy, counseling, and shelter. Results of the evaluation provide a ringing endorsement for the work of Illinois's sexual assault and domestic violence agencies and point out areas in which services could be improved.

This project unfolded in roughly two phases: evaluation development and evaluation implementation. The first phase of the project included developing evaluation objectives, measurement tools, and data collection procedures; providing workshops for program staff introducing them to evaluation; creating a training manual for evaluating sexual assault and domestic violence programs; and field-testing the evaluation measures repeatedly. In the second phase, sampling plans were finalized, evaluation measures were distributed throughout the state, agencies were trained to collect the data using the evaluation measures and to use the evaluation findings within their own organizations, and one fiscal year's worth of data was collected and analyzed. (For a detailed chronology of the project, see our Web site: www.uic.edu/depts/psch/idhs.)

EVALUATION APPROACH

Several considerations shaped the approach we took to this evaluation. First, the state department of human services initiated this project with specific needs in mind. For example, the state needed to assess all programs serving victimized women, requiring the evaluation of more than 80 sites across Illinois. In addition, because the state wanted to combine and compare outcomes between programs, we needed to develop standardized evaluation instruments. However, program implementation (i.e., how the services are delivered) differed between programs. We adopted an approach to evaluating multiple programs with similar goals but different activities called *cluster evaluation*. The W. K. Kellogg Foundation developed this approach to evaluate "clusters" of projects either because they were funded by the same source or because the programs addressed the same topic (Worthen, Sanders, & Fitzpatrick, 1997). Cluster evaluation approaches (a) are driven by questions that deal with priority issues of funding officials; (b) identify common information needed on all projects in order to provide a composite overview of the overall success or failure of the cluster; and (c) outline methods to collect such data.

In 1991, the W. K. Kellogg Foundation (Worthen et al., 1997) identified four key characteristics of a good cluster evaluation. First, it should include the identification of common threads and themes across a group of projects. Second, the evaluation seeks to learn not only what happened with respect to a group of projects but also why those things happened. Third, it happens in a collaborative way that allows all players to contribute. Finally, the relationship between organizations and external evaluators remains confidential. Although our project was not able to entirely meet these criteria (particularly the last one), we did use frequent communication, focus groups, and training workshops to involve as many program staff as possible in all evaluation activities.

A second consideration was the mixed opinions about evaluation among the staff of the programs to be evaluated. Some staff mistrusted the state, the university, and research in general, creating considerable resistance to the evaluation. We adopted a collaborative approach to give program staff a significant role in determining the objectives and methods of the evaluation. We also selected a collaborative approach because we think it produces better research—agency staff know far more about their services and clients than we do. Participatory evaluation methods are consistent with cluster evaluation.

Ultimately, the representatives of the agencies were key to making this statewide initiative a success. Moreover, programs staff participation in all stages of the evaluation allowed them to ensure appropriate protection of their clients' safety and confidentiality.

CONSIDERATIONS IN EVALUATING DOMESTIC VIOLENCE AND SEXUAL ASSAULT SERVICES

Several topics present practical concerns to both evaluators and providers of services to victimized women: (a) politics, (b) confidentiality, (c) the safety and welfare of service recipients, (d) organizational resources, (e) literacy and language, and (f) research design. Discussion of each of these issues will be illustrated by examples from our work in Illinois. Finally, we present the most important lessons we learned doing this project.

Politics

As mentioned throughout this book, evaluators must be sensitive to issues of politics when developing evaluation procedures for services to victims of gender-based violence. Because they were often founded by women's rights activists and frequently are rooted in politicized social change agendas, domestic violence and sexual assault service delivery organizations may be especially wary of the role that evaluation could play in allocating scarce resources. Therefore, evaluation efforts that require the cooperation of frontline workers should begin by negotiating how to share control of both the process and the results of the evaluation (see Chapter 2). Without early, frequent, and open discussions about the purpose of the evaluation, as well as possible ramifications on resources or service delivery, evaluators of domestic violence and sexual assault services might find themselves working *against* rather than *with* the programs they are trying to evaluate.

The first political issue that we encountered was the need to distinguish sexual assault services and providers from those of domestic violence. The funders requested that we create one set of standardized outcome measures for both types of agencies. In early discussions between service providers and the research team, the services (e.g., hotline, counseling, advocacy) and the intended outcomes (e.g., safety, support, increased information) appeared to be similar across both sexual assault and domestic violence services. Thus, initially we created one set of measures to be used in all programs. However, in Illinois, and in many states, these two service provider communities are separate entities, with different histories, and are organized into different power structures and coalitions (see Chapter 1 for an overview of these ideas). Some programs may be concerned about how merging the issues of domestic violence and sexual assault together might force them to compete for the same funding opportunities. This political issue shaped both the design and the implementation of the evaluation in that we divided the original single set of standardized measures into two separate sets of measures, one specifically for domestic violence services and the other for sexual assault services. Although the hotline and counseling measures remained similar, advocacy measures differed considerably because of differences in advocacy services between domestic violence and sexual assault.

Another political issue was the perceived conflict between evaluation practice and the philosophy behind advocacy services in certain settings. Advocates were concerned that asking evaluation questions of clients interfered with developing supportive relationships and shifted the focus of advocacy interactions from client to organizational needs, thereby eliminating the unique feature of their services, that is, to be totally client centered. For crisis hotline and brief criminal justice and medical advocacy services, for example, the essence of the service providers' work was to build trust with and reinstate a sense of control to survivors. In our evaluation design, we tried to address potential conflict between the mission of advocacy services and evaluation work by limiting the number of questions asked of brief advocacy and hotline clients and making those questions as simple and natural sounding as possible. At the conclusion of one year of data collection, we recommended to the state that hotline and brief advocacy not be evaluated at the point of service. This was based on our desire not to interfere with the development of trust and rapport between advocates and clients and, as discussed below, the safety and welfare of clients. Also, the large volume of these services, and the hectic situations in which they were delivered, made data collection difficult. Furthermore, we found no significant statistical differences between responses to questions about the hotline when asked as part of the counseling intake procedure than when asked at the end of a crisis phone call.

Some programs had difficulties with the evaluation procedures for counseling. Counselors explained to us that building rapport and retaining regular contact with some clients was one of their greatest challenges in service delivery. Some counselors did not want to administer the "before-counseling" survey at the intake meeting because they saw initiating the often tenuous process of building trust with their clients as the primary purpose of that first meeting. They feared that requiring clients to fill out rather lengthy surveys before they even met their counselors may obstruct this process. In response, we adapted the evaluation procedures so that counselors were instructed to have their clients fill out the before-counseling survey as soon as possible, but they could choose when, within the first two sessions, it was most appropriate to administer the survey.

Confidentiality

In this project, state laws as well as federal guidelines on the protection for human research subjects regulate the confidentiality of the recipients of domestic violence and sexual assault services. When collecting any type of information that could be used to identify a client (e.g., address, phone number, date of birth), evaluators need to ensure that they do not put clients at risk of harm and that they do not violate the law. In addition, to obtain useful information about weaknesses in services, clients need to feel safe that their identity or their relationship with the organizations will be protected and that the feedback they provide will not be used to harm the agency or to prevent them from obtaining services. For these reasons, often the best choice is to collect data anonymously. When it is necessary to collect data with identifiers (e.g., for before and after evaluation designs), the identification method must keep identities confidential. We grappled with issues of confidentiality in evaluating many of the services provided to survivors of domestic violence or sexual assault.

For example, counseling clients filled out forms before and after counseling sessions and we measured the amount of change they experienced. To do so, we had to match each woman's pre- and post-counseling forms. Therefore, we needed some way to identify her. But in doing so, we had to protect clients' confidentiality on two levels: as crime victims and as research subjects. In Illinois, legal protections for recipients of domestic violence and sexual assault services require their names or any other identifying information to remain confidential. These laws were instituted to prevent information from being used against victims in a court of law. Agencies were concerned that defense attorneys might subpoena completed evaluation forms, which contained sensitive information. To prevent this, the completed evaluation forms could not remain in case files. Therefore, to match clients' before and after counseling measures, we had to create a unique code that did not use names, social security number, date of birth, phone numbers, or any other identifying information.

Federal policies also protect the safety and confidentiality of human research subjects. This affected not only the implementation of our before and after counseling evaluation measures but the shelter evaluation as well. Here, the concern is that a woman's ability to receive ongoing services should not be jeopardized by her responses on the evaluation forms. To encourage honest responses, clients' anonymity had to be secured. This was accomplished by counseling and shelter clients filling out their own evaluation forms, sealing them in an envelope, placing them in a drop box, and having forms sent directly to the evaluators for analysis. Although this process protected the women as research subjects, it was very frustrating for counselors who wanted to use information from the evaluation to better address clients' needs in counseling or shelter programs.

Protecting Confidentiality and
Working with Institutional Review Boards

Two months into the implementation year of our project, all human subject research at the University of Illinois at Chicago was suspended temporarily because of violations of procedures to protect human subjects in research. Although no violations occurred in our project, our work was stopped until the university could revise its oversight procedures. This occurrence highlighted for us the importance of informed consent when conducting program evaluation.

Evaluating agencies' services requires that information be obtained from clients who receive those services. Obtaining that information must not, as we have emphasized, put clients at risk or harm them in any way. To ensure that clients are knowledgeable and voluntary participants in evaluation research, many organizations require that clients actively consent to participate. In many organizations, "institutional review boards" oversee research to make sure that participants are fully informed and that their participation is voluntary. All research procedures involving human beings must be described in detail and approved by the review board. The review board may require that participants sign a consent form to show that the research has been explained to them, that they understand the research, and that they have agreed to participate.

Typically, consent forms include explanations of the research and what will happen to participants. Consent forms are supposed to include a description of the direct benefits of the research, the possible harm from participation (even if that harm is unlikely), the name and telephone number of the researcher, and other information. They are supposed to be written in clear language that is free of jargon. In practice, however, including all that required information could result in a multipage consent form that confuses participants.

Although intended to protect research participants, signed consent forms may be problematic in research with women who have been victimized. Many agencies promise clients that their names will not be known to anyone outside the agency. Having clients sign a consent form that may be sent to a researcher outside the agency may violate agencies' policies of privacy and confidentiality for their clients. In some cases, such as in Illinois, provisions of state laws protecting the confidentiality of victims prohibit sending signed consent forms outside the agency. For cases in which harm may come from a breach of confidentiality, review boards may agree to clients' verbal consent (and waive the required documentation of signed consent) after the research has been explained to them via an information sheet (see example in Appendixes A and B). After lengthy negotiation with our university's human subjects review board and our participating agencies, we used this method for ensuring informed consent of evaluation participants.

Safety and Welfare of Service Recipients

It is important for evaluators to recognize that the services offered to survivors of violence are delivered to women who may be in crisis and in danger. Evaluation should not be done when a woman is in crisis or danger. Rather, the attention of the service provider should focus on helping the client. To the extent that evaluation detracts from the service providers' ability to help clients in crisis, the evaluation undermines one of its prime directives: Do not endanger clients to collect data. Even when no crisis is apparent, each evaluation contact must be carefully designed to ensure the safety and welfare of victims.

For example, although it might be possible to evaluate hotline calls by contacting callers at a later date, we decided not to contact callers for evaluation purposes because we felt the safety and privacy of clients was more important than the quality of evaluation data. Contacting a victim at home to ask evaluation questions may place her at risk of harm because people in her home, and possibly her assailant or abuser, may not know that she has sought outside help for abuse. Someone else in the home might open follow-up letters, answer follow-up calls, or hear messages on an answering machine, thereby violating her privacy and potentially placing her in danger. Furthermore, the nature of the hotline service is anonymous, and even if it were safe to do so, asking callers to disclose their name or contact information to the hotline worker would undermine a central tenet of the hotline and may discourage women from using services in the future.

Concerns about the safety and welfare of clients determined how we decided to evaluate hotline telephone calls. We developed a short set of questions and two formats for asking them of clients: Either the hotline worker would ask them at the end of the phone contact or a staff member would give the questions in written form to clients who came in for counseling as part of the counseling intake paperwork. In addition, to ensure that no hotline caller was asked evaluation questions while in crisis, the format used for asking questions at the end of the call contained the following instruction: "If the caller is in crisis or you think it would upset the caller further, do not ask Questions 1 through 4. Instead, go directly to Question 5." As can be seen in Appendix A, Questions 1 through 4 are the evaluation questions asked directly of the client, and Question 5 begins the section that the hotline worker fills out after the call is completed. In this way, if the service provider determined that the client was in a state of crisis or that asking evaluation questions may add to her distress, the provider did not ask the evaluation questions and she indicated the reason on the measure. As it turned out, results from the two hotline evaluation methods were statistically identical, further supporting our decision to eliminate evaluation of hotline calls at the point of contact. Similar instructions were included on brief advocacy evaluation measures because those clients were also frequently in crisis. Sexual assault service providers were more vocal than domestic violence service providers in their concern about administering evaluations to women who might be in crisis, perhaps because more of their clients are in crisis when they request services.

At times, service providers disagreed about whether evaluation procedures might jeopardize the safety and welfare of their clients. For example, in the evaluation of counseling, many sexual assault agencies wanted to measure the change in certain symptoms such as feeling bad about yourself, feelings of guilt, or feeling like injuring or hurting yourself, in order to demonstrate the effectiveness of their counseling services in reducing rape-related distress. Domestic violence agencies, however, were concerned that answering such questions would make women feel as though something was wrong with them. Furthermore, if the confidentiality procedures described in the previous section were ever breached, clients' answers to these questions might be used against women in custody battles. Domestic violence service providers felt that these risks to clients' welfare were too great to justify including the items. Because the sexual assault and domestic violence evaluations had been separated, we eliminated the items measuring distress from the domestic violence counseling evaluation.

Organizational Resources

The availability of organizational resources must inform any evaluation plan. Evaluation requires time, space, staff, and office supplies; each of these requires money. It is imperative that proper resources are available for each stage of the evaluation process: developing the plan, collecting the data, managing the data, and putting the results to use. Evaluators should also be aware of data collection that programs may be doing concurrently and try to make sure that evaluation questions do not duplicate data collected with existing paperwork.

The agencies we were working with were already collecting a lot of data required by funders and were resistant to collecting more information that would not directly benefit their organizations. To be efficient and foster goodwill with those collecting data, we limited the number of questions we asked; we kept all of the evaluation procedures and forms as simple as possible; and we did not duplicate other data collection efforts. As a result of the collaboration between our evaluation team and the service providers, many agencies were able to use this evaluation for those requested by other funding agencies.

Sometimes our best intentions to keep data collection procedures reasonable given the other demands on service providers were trumped by circumstances beyond our control. For example, the hectic pace of the court system pitted service delivery against evaluation procedures. In other words, some court advocates noted that they did not have enough time, space, or staff to do the evaluation without sacrificing the quality of the advocacy services. Thus, some advocates independently decided to change the format of the measure from interview to a self-administered survey so that they could hand the evaluation to clients to fill out while advocates completed other legal paperwork.

Literacy and Language

When designing evaluation measures, consideration must be given to the literacy level of the population. Introductions to the evaluation process as well as the questions and answer choices should be modeled on advocates' language in these interactions. For example, although we refer to the rape crisis centers and domestic violence shelters as "agencies," service providers and clients do not. Service providers suggested substituting the name of their program where the word "agency" appeared in our original measures. Literacy was one of the considerations that shaped our decision to use an interview, rather than survey, format for the hotline and advocacy measures; although, as mentioned earlier, one negative consequence of this choice was that busy advocates, such as those who assist women in obtaining orders of protection at the court, did not have enough time to read the evaluation questions aloud to each client.

Given the dynamics of rape and domestic violence, service providers were especially vigilant that word choices did not convey victim-blaming sentiment. For example, they suggested "my situation" or "the assault/abuse" instead of "my problem" in the wording of one question. For fear of insinuating that a woman is responsible for preventing future rapes, sexual assault providers asked us to eliminate the following item from the counseling measure: "My counselor helped me figure out ways to make my present situation safer."

Translation of measures from one language to another requires sensitivity to idiomatic expressions within the language that could create confusion for clients. Because agencies served different Spanish-speaking populations (e.g., Mexican and Puerto Rican) in Illinois, we encountered problems with the translation of our measures from English to Spanish. Spanish-speaking service providers often had to take extra time to explain the nuances of the Spanish words used in the consent form and survey questions. Creating both English and other language versions of a measure simultaneously may prevent the use in English of idiomatic phrases or words that are difficult to translate.

Research Design

Politics, confidentiality, safety and welfare of clients, organizational resources, and language and literacy considerations shape research design. Other issues that will affect the precision and validity of the data collected are data sources, the timing and sequencing of the evaluation, the interviewer, and the wording of the measures.

Evaluation of the brief advocacy services provides an example of how research design can affect the validity of evaluation results. After much consideration of confidentiality and literacy issues, we decided to have providers administer the evaluation to their clients at the conclusion of the service rather than have women complete forms themselves. This opened the possibility that the results of our evaluation of brief advocacy are biased because clients who are asked evaluation questions by their service provider may be inclined toward positive feedback so as not to appear impolite or ungrateful. (As noted above, sometimes advocates decided to have women fill out their own forms if they were pressed for time.) The same bias was present for hotline evaluations administered by hotline workers at the end of the call.

Designing the evaluation of a shelter raised another challenge. Women stay in shelters for varying amounts of time. Shelter workers worried that a few of the long-term residents might give the same evaluation information multiple times, skewing the results toward those residents' opinions. To prevent the voices of long-term residents from overpowering those who remained for a shorter time, our design needed to ensure that each woman evaluated the shelter only once during her stay. Originally, our design had shelter evaluations administered every 14 days to all residents present at "house meetings" so that we could determine whether length of stay influenced evaluation outcomes. However, to avoid the concern of bias raised by service providers, the surveys were still passed out every second week, but the staff instructed residents not to complete an evaluation if they had already completed one since arriving at the shelter.

Another design issue we encountered when evaluating domestic violence services was distinguishing services delivered in the shelter, sometimes by shelter staff, from shelter living. To prevent conflating the effects of advocacy and counseling (services delivered to both residents and nonresidents) with the effects of living in the shelter, we separated the benefits of the shelter living environment from counseling and advocacy. The shelter evaluation only asked questions that related to a sense of physical and emotional safety and comfort in the shelter residence.

Yet another design issue emerged in the evaluation of advocacy services. In our discussions with providers, it became apparent that agencies differed in drawing the line between brief and extended advocacy. To address this, we decided to divide advocacy evaluation tools into "brief advocacy" and "extended advocacy." The agencies used a brief advocacy evaluation form at the end of the first advocacy session with each person, and completed an extended advocacy evaluation form with each client who completed an average number of sessions (individualized by agency). The variation in advocacy services at the different programs, unfortunately, precluded us from using a before and after evaluation design.

LESSONS LEARNED

We have learned a lot during the course of this project. Some of what we learned will apply only to multisite evaluation initiatives whereas some will apply only to evaluations of services for victimized women. What we learned about collaboration, however, may apply across many different kinds of evaluation projects. The first two lessons learned are that (a) it is difficult to standardize outcomes across programs; and (b) the goals assessed in outcome evaluations must not hold victims or agencies responsible for the incidence of sexual or domestic violence. The third lesson is that given the nature of violence against women, evaluating sexual assault or domestic violence services requires sensitivity to the needs of survivors of sexual and domestic violence. Finally, we learned that participatory methods and our collaboration with the domestic violence and sexual assault programs increased the organizational evaluation capacity of the participating agencies and made this evaluation possible.

Difficulties in Standardizing Outcomes Across Multiple Programs

Developing generic measures for programs with varying resources, geographical locations, clientele, and organizational structures was difficult. Although objectives of hotline, advocacy, counseling, and shelter services were similar in programs across the state, the organizational and community context in which the services were delivered, and sometimes the program activities implemented, were different. We developed acceptable generalized measures for these five services, but we do not necessarily recommend standardized measures for more varied programs like volunteer training, community education, or services for children. Because this evaluation was a statewide initiative, it necessarily included diverse communities (e.g., urban and rural). Our evaluation emphasized commonality across programs at the expense of accounting for unique activities or contextual factors. Furthermore, whereas standardized outcome measures may identify differences between programs, it may be difficult for data collected using these measures to *explain* those differences.

We suggest that, whenever possible, outcome assessments such as the one we developed be accompanied by more detailed process evaluation that documents the specifics of how services were delivered. In the case of Illinois, the programs we evaluated already participated in another project implemented by the Illinois Criminal Justice Information Authority (ICJIA) that provides to the state descriptive process information about each service contact. Combining these two data sets may answer some questions raised by the evaluation outcome data.

Evaluation Objectives Must Not
Hold Survivors Responsible for Violence

State administrators requested that we examine long-term indicators of the effect of domestic violence and sexual assault services in addition to measuring outcomes on service recipients. At the outset of the project, they cited examining changes in infant mortality rates as exemplary of long-term outcomes of prenatal care programs (such as the Women, Infants, and Children program) and challenged our team to develop similar long-term indicators for domestic violence and sexual assault services. Determining appropriate long-term outcome indicators for the success of these programs, however, posed a serious problem.

Although many of the agencies evaluated in this project consider a major long-term goal of their work to change societal attitudes toward victimized women and prevent violence against women, most of their resources go toward services provided to victims—which do not necessarily change societal attitudes nor prevent future violence. Many of the agencies' programs that provide services to victims do not directly address the source, or perpetrators, of the violence. They seek, rather, to reduce the trauma associated with victimization, to minimize the stigma associated with being a victim, and to encourage survivors' use of healthy management and safety strategies. Victims' final outcomes, such as empowerment, recovery, or revictimization, are affected by multiple factors at the community level and agency services are one small part of their experiences.

A feminist analysis of violence against women places the responsibility for the violence on perpetrators and social norms. In contrast, a logic model that holds programs for victims responsible for decreasing rates of violence would shift blame for not stopping the abuse onto victims or agencies. The feminist perspective, for example, implies that it is illogical to monitor the number of reported rapes or domestic violence convictions as outcomes of services to victimized women. An important task for participants in this evaluation project, then, was to incorporate feminist perspectives about violence against women into the evaluation objectives and outcome measures. We did not develop a long-term indicator of the success of domestic violence and sexual assault programs; such an indicator might be change among members of a community in attitudes that blame women for the violence they experience.

In developing measures, we considered carefully how logic models, evaluation objectives, and even wording of items could attribute blame to victims. Throughout the development of the evaluation plan, representatives from the agencies changed our wording choices to clarify that the victim was not responsible for the sexual or domestic violence. For example, many counselors work with clients who blame themselves for the abuse they experienced. Thus, in the counseling measure, domestic violence service providers asked us to add the item: "Violence is not just a personal problem, but a social problem" to reflect the change they hope to make on their clients' self-blaming attitudes.

Services to Victims Require Sensitivity in Evaluation

Many service providers expressed concerns about collecting information from women who may be in states of crisis when they use services. Service providers insisted that evaluation efforts must not put recipients of the services—especially when they are in crisis or vulnerable—at risk of further harm or distress. Thus, our measures of hotline calls and advocacy emphasized the use of information that could be collected from service providers themselves, such as how many referrals were provided. When we recommended collecting information from clients, we made every effort to make the questions brief and unintrusive. Ideally, for evaluation purposes, a person independent of the agency should contact a client to ask about the effectiveness of services. But, in order to protect clients' confidentiality and safety, we suggested that service providers trained to deal with issues of sexual and domestic violence administer the evaluation procedures.

200

200

CASH BRICKS

Fleischmann

200 PLAYMONEY NO CASH VALUE 2014

R14 14000

MOST AUTHENTIC PLAYMONEY

200

200

200

200

X0064398619 4

PLAYMONEY NOTE
X0064398619 4

WWW.CASHBRICKS.NET

200 CASH BRICKS

200

As mentioned earlier in this chapter, the decision to have service providers ask some of the evaluation questions raised a second major concern of program representatives. Service providers were worried that asking questions of victimized women, often in states of immediate or chronic crisis, would distort the interactions with clients who have often experienced significant trauma and loss of control. Program staff members hope to reinstate feelings of control and autonomy in women's lives. Some agencies felt that taking control of an advocacy contact or a counseling session to determine the efficacy of programs clashed with their service philosophy and undermined their goal of giving the client control over her services and her recovery.

These concerns from agency representatives guided our recommendations about conducting future evaluations of domestic violence and sexual assault programs. For example, staff at one rape crisis center shared with us an unfortunate example of how evaluation added to one victim's confusion and crisis. A rape victim did not understand the evaluation questions being asked of her in the emergency room following the rape exam. After the advocate explained to her the purpose of the questions, the client told the advocate: "I'm sorry, I must not be smart enough to answer those questions." Clearly, when evaluating emergency services such as these, the evaluation must not add to victims' distress, vulnerability, feelings of low self-worth (as in the preceding example), or self-blame. Ultimately, we recommended to the state that emergency services such as crisis hotline or brief advocacy not be evaluated during the interaction while women are in crisis.

"Mandated Collaboration" Can Increase Evaluation Capacity

Because this project emphasized collaboration between different stakeholder groups to arrive at mutually satisfactory decisions about the evaluation, the stakeholder groups had the opportunity to learn a great deal from one another. We, as researchers, learned about the nature of advocacy services, for example, and how and why evaluation may interrupt the goals of those services. The participating agencies learned how to do evaluations in their agencies. As can be expected in a large project such as this one, the amount of learning about evaluation that happened varied among agencies. One problem was that we were not able to collaborate with all agencies equally. Not all agencies had the resources or interest in collaborating with us. In many cases, we relied on the volunteerism of agencies in determining whose voices would be heard. Other projects may be able to provide incentives and resources to cover collaboration costs of time and energy. However, for better or for worse—and our hope is for better—each participating agency had the experience of collecting evaluation data from their staff and their program participants.

Throughout this process of mandated evaluation, state funders, the evaluation research team, and the agency representatives relied on each other to navigate the decision points entailed in a good evaluation. First, we asked the agencies to think about the various services that they provide and consider which of those services were most important to evaluate. In so doing, the representatives of the agencies helped us to assess the evaluability of each of their programs (see Chapter 4 for additional description of evaluability assessments). Second, we asked agencies to identify the desired impacts of each of their programs on program participants, the first step in creating a goal-based evaluation plan. Although our evaluation team "translated" the desired impacts into measurable outcome objectives, service providers were given structured opportunities to provide feedback on the evaluation objectives we developed. The process of responding to our evaluation objectives, often suggesting alternative objectives for ones they did not like, provided agency representatives practice in developing measurable objectives. Similarly, their item-by-item analysis of our evaluation measures provided them hands-on experience in measurement development while improving the measures considerably.

Most important, agency staff learned to collect data, which was awkward for many of them. But they did it: Every participating agency asked themselves and their clients questions about the services they provide. Many of the agencies were highly resistant to this part of the evaluation, perhaps for reasons that were more related to the process of asking than to the answers they received. Some staff felt uncomfortable asking the evaluation questions; others felt it changed their role from that of helper to evaluator. Although many agency representatives would still prefer to not ask the questions at all, or to have someone else ask the questions, they now possess the knowledge that they are capable of doing it. This increased organizational capacity allows agency representatives to consider interview and survey methods as options for future evaluations or other information-gathering missions. It is likely that some of these agencies would never even have considered these options if they had not been encouraged (i.e., mandated) by the funders to participate in the evaluation process.

One can imagine an external team of evaluators, not trained in working with victimized women, who would conduct all evaluation interviews and surveys and hand the data straight to the state representatives without involving the program staff at all. Although this would certainly alleviate the program staff of the additional burdens of collecting data, program staff would learn nothing about their programs, or their own personal service provisions, until the evaluator shared the data with the agency representatives. Furthermore, evaluators untrained in the needs of survivors of violence may unwittingly put women in danger or exacerbate abuse. In contrast to that scenario, it is likely that the evaluation project described here resulted in an increased capacity for understanding, conducting, and using program evaluation within the participating agencies.

Changes over the course of this project in agency representatives' primary concerns provide evidence of their increasing evaluation capacity. When the idea of the evaluation project was introduced to the organizations, representatives of sexual assault and domestic violence agencies first voiced some of the concerns that have continued to be issued throughout the evaluation: How will the evaluation findings be used? Will negative results be used in a punitive way (e.g., to discontinue funding)? Will agencies be provided additional resources to carry out this evaluation? What is the purpose of the evaluation? Who will be responsible for implementation? In the beginning, the concerns about the evaluation were practical and inextricably linked to funding concerns. After two years' effort, their concerns were less likely to be about "How will this evaluation affect our funding?" and more about "Is this evaluation collecting valid, meaningful data in a way that will allow us to improve our programs?"

Over time, the major concerns of agency representatives shifted away from the relationship between evaluation and funding to the relationship between evaluation and the feminist model of service delivery. Specifically, service providers challenged our research team to think about whether it is appropriate to ask questions of women in crisis situations and, if so, when and how it should be done. Some agencies continued to express hesitation and unease about the additional paperwork burden and the purpose of the evaluation, but many more wondered about the impact of evaluation on service delivery and whether they will be able to use evaluation data to improve the lives of women following violence. We consider these concerns—even though they may raise questions about the evaluation we developed— as a measure of successful transference of the concepts and value of evaluation to women's advocates in community-based organizations.

FUTURE DIRECTIONS

Our experience in this evaluation suggests several principles for future design and implementation of evaluation for domestic violence and sexual assault services. First, evaluation cannot compromise clients' safety and welfare. If clients will be asked directly about their experiences, trained and experienced people must do so in a sensitive manner. The expertise of advocates and direct service providers is critical to a balanced evaluation that respects clients' needs while simultaneously gathering useful information about services.

Based on our experiences and the empirical data gathered through both quantitative and qualitative methods, we would recommend not collecting evaluation data in certain circumstances. First, in emergency situations or situations in which the client is in crisis, we strongly recommend not asking evaluation questions of clients. Our data indicate that advocates reported clients' discomfort with doing evaluation at these times and clients often chose not to participate at these times. Second, the implementation of evaluation procedures should interfere as little as possible with the development of trust and rapport between client and service provider. From the service provider's perspective, evaluation at these times can undermine the purpose of the service by drawing attention away from the client's needs and onto the agency's needs.

If we had the opportunity to redo this project, we would do four things (at least) again. First, we would involve service providers in all phases of evaluation development and implementation. This aspect of our project was crucial to its success. It is especially important to have advocates review all questions for wording so that the resulting questions and introduction scripts sound natural and are understandable to clients; nobody knows the client population as well as the service providers. Furthermore, service providers can provide useful information when determining the feasibility of implementation in specific settings such as, for example, the courts.

Second, we would provide motivation for domestic violence and sexual assault service providers to become invested in the evaluation process. Evaluators should try to develop evaluation with service providers' needs in mind. In other words, the evaluation should be useful to service providers' purposes, such as to secure additional funding or target program weaknesses for improvement. Then, the results of evaluation should be shared with agencies in a format that is useful to them, whether that be primary data (e.g., verbatim quotes of clients) or results of quantitative analyses such as percentages or means.

Third, we would ensure that agencies have adequate resources. Evaluation requires money, paper, time, people, and space. Often, evaluation components are required of community-based agencies where these resources are scarce, making evaluation a burden. Gathering information about current data collection and evaluation materials might help identify ways to reduce burdensome paperwork and incur goodwill. Because they collect funds from various funding sources, many agencies are already required to collect certain types of information and conduct evaluation of specific outcomes; when possible, new evaluation activities should be integrated into existing ones.

Finally, given the special needs of victimized women, we would always allow the service provider to assess whether the evaluation is appropriate or to terminate the evaluation if the client becomes distressed, confused, or frustrated by the evaluation procedures. We would continue to operate under the basic principle that the service delivery component of the work is more important than the evaluation component.

The issues discussed in this chapter go beyond our particular project to evaluation projects more generally. A successful evaluation requires the commitment to understanding the agency you are working with, its history, and its micro- and macrolevel politics. In the area of violence against women, evaluators must always design the evaluation with the concern for victims' safety. Giving this concern top priority will reduce the risk for participants and may build trust between evaluators and agency staff and volunteers. The confidentiality issues that we encountered highlight the importance of developing evaluation protocols that meet both state statutes for crime victims and ethical standards of internal review boards. Issues of organizational resources are similar in many nonprofit agencies and, across the board, evaluators need to be conscious of potential discrepancies between available resources and workload. In the area of language and literacy, evaluators must be conscious of not only developing measures that are easy to answer for people at all literacy levels but also to design introductions and instructions to sound as natural as possible. The more "natural" the language, the more the evaluation will be in line with the mission of the agency. As this chapter suggests, successful evaluations occur when evaluators join forces with service providers in a sensitive and responsible manner.

KEY POINTS

- In evaluating services in Illinois, service providers were crucial in identifying measurable performance goals, developing the structure and wording of evaluation measures, and determining reasonable data collection plans.
- The evaluation research team developed an infrastructure of evaluation resources for agencies by creating manuals, sponsoring training workshops, creating a Web site, and giving data and results in usable formats.

- Political tensions are inherent in funder-mandated evaluation projects but may be minimized by including stakeholders in open discussions about the purpose of the evaluation, the process of data collection, the use of the results, and being responsive to the program representatives' concerns, feedback, and suggestions.
- Special confidentiality concerns exist when working with survivors of sexual and domestic violence; evaluators of sexual assault and domestic violence services need to ensure that confidentiality procedures protect evaluation participants both as both victims of crime and as research subjects.
- A range of emotional, physical, and psychological consequences is associated with the experience of sexual and domestic violence that will influence how evaluators collect data from survivors; evaluations should not be done when clients are in states of crisis and the evaluation procedures should not place women seeking services at risk of danger or additional distress.
- Programs offering sexual assault and domestic violence services are likely to lack the organizational resources necessary to conduct a quality evaluation; evaluation efforts should start by assessing needs and obtaining staff, time, space, equipment, and supplies necessary for the evaluation.
- The wording of evaluations measures should reflect the language of service providers, using terms and phrasing suited to the literacy levels, ethnicity, and cultural customs of the clients.
- The nature of sexual assault and domestic violence services, which are often one-time contacts, crisis-based, or taking place in community settings like courtrooms, may restrict the research design options available to evaluators.
- The context of social movements (sexual assault versus domestic violence) and the geography of the city, neighborhood, and organization greatly influence service delivery methods, making standardized outcome measures difficult to develop when using collaborative methods.
- Outcome objectives must be carefully structured so as to not hold victims of violence responsible for decreasing violence. Every evaluation contact with a survivor of sexual assault or domestic violence must be carefully designed so as to not harm survivors or undermine the purpose of the services.
- Participation in evaluation planning and data collection may increase evaluation capacity among domestic violence and sexual assault service programs.

Appendix A

Evaluation Measures for Domestic Violence Services

DOMESTIC VIOLENCE
INFORMATION SHEET
BEFORE COUNSELING SURVEY

We are asking you to participate in a research project to help us improve our services. We want to know how helpful our counseling services are, so we are asking all those who receive counseling to fill out this questionnaire. Some questions ask about past experiences of abuse and about how you are feeling emotionally. You might find some of these questions upsetting. Your participation is voluntary; you do not have to do this and you may stop at any time. Your decision whether or not to participate will not affect your relationship with our agency. About 5,000 people who receive counseling services from agencies in Illinois will fill out this questionnaire and your answers will be combined with theirs into one report. Your answers will be kept confidential and your name or other identifying information will not appear in any report. This research may bring no direct benefit to you but it will enable us to improve our service to all our clients.

You have been given an envelope for the questionnaire. If you agree to participate, when you are done with the questionnaire, put it in the envelope, seal the envelope, and put it in the drop box. We will then send it, with those from other people, to be analyzed by qualified researchers at the University of Illinois at Chicago. No one from this agency will see your individual responses and there is no way that anyone can link your name with your responses. You should not put your name on the questionnaire.

If you have any questions, please ask them now. If you have questions later, you may contact the researcher, Stephanie Riger, at the University of Illinois at Chicago at 312-413-2300. If you have any questions about your rights as a research subject, you may call the Office for Protection of Research Subjects at 312-996-1711. If you decide to participate, keep this information sheet for your records.

_____
Password

BEFORE COUNSELING SURVEY

Thank you for taking the time to answer these questions. We want to know how helpful our counseling services are to you, so your feedback is very important to us. Your answers will be kept confidential. Nothing you say will affect the services that you receive.

PLEASE DO NOT PUT YOUR NAME ON THIS SURVEY

1. How often are the following statements true for you? For each statement in rows "a" through "h," please circle *one* number.

		Never	*Rarely*	*Sometimes*	*Often*	*Always*
a.	I have someone I can turn to for helpful advice about a problem	1	2	3	4	5
b.	I have someone who would help me in times of trouble	1	2	3	4	5
c.	I trust my ability to solve difficult problems	1	2	3	4	5
d.	I am confident about the decisions that I make	1	2	3	4	5
e.	I feel like I'm in control of my own life	1	2	3	4	5
f.	I have ways to help myself when I feel troubled	1	2	3	4	5
g.	I know the abuse was not my fault	1	2	3	4	5
h.	I am able to talk about my thoughts and feelings about the abuse	1	2	3	4	5

2. Have you ever called our crisis hotline in the past?

     Yes .... 1→ (ANSWER QUESTIONS 3 TO 5)

     No.. 2→ (STOP, TURN IN SURVEY)

     Don't know .... 3→ (STOP, TURN IN SURVEY)

3. How many times have you called our crisis hotline?

     1-3 times... 1

     4-6 times... 2

     More than 6 times 3

     Don't know 99

4. After calling the crisis hotline, how much more information did you have about the choices available to you? Would you say you had . . .

     A lot more information, ... 4

     Somewhat more information, ... 3

     A little more information, or 2

     No more information? 1

5. How much support did you get from the crisis hotline? Would you say that the crisis hotline gave you . . .

     A lot of support, ... 4

     Some support, ... 3

     A little support, or 2

     No support at all? 1

Thank you again for taking the time to answer these
questions. Your opinion is very important to us so
that we can improve our services.

DOMESTIC VIOLENCE
INFORMATION SHEET
COUNSELING SURVEY

We are asking you to participate in a research project to help us improve our services. We want to know how helpful our counseling services are, so we are asking all those who receive counseling to fill out this questionnaire. Some questions ask about past experiences of abuse and about how you are feeling emotionally. You might find some of these questions upsetting. Your participation is voluntary; you do not have to do this and you may stop at any time. Your decision whether or not to participate will not affect your relationship with our agency. About 5,000 people who receive counseling services from agencies in Illinois will fill out this questionnaire and your answers will be combined with theirs into one report. Your answers will be kept confidential and your name or other identifying information will not appear in any report. This research may bring no direct benefit to you, but it will enable us to improve our service to all our clients.

You have been given an envelope for the questionnaire. If you agree to participate, when you are done with the questionnaire, put it in the envelope, seal the envelope, and put it in the drop box. We will then send it, with those from other people, to be analyzed by qualified researchers at the University of Illinois at Chicago. No one from this agency will see your individual responses and there is no way that anyone can link your name with your responses. You should not put your name on the questionnaire.

If you have any questions, please ask them now. If you have questions later, you may contact the researcher, Stephanie Riger, at the University of Illinois at Chicago at 312-413-2300. If you have any questions about your rights as a research subject, you may call the Office for Protection of Research Subjects at 312-996-1711. If you decide to participate, keep this information sheet for your records.

Password

COUNSELING SURVEY

Thank you for taking the time to answer these questions. We want to know how helpful our counseling services are to you, so your feedback is very important to us. Your answers will be kept confidential. Nothing you say will affect the services that you receive.

PLEASE DO NOT PUT YOUR NAME ON THIS SURVEY

1. How often are the following statements true for you? For each statement in rows "a" through "h," please circle *one* number.

		Never	*Rarely*	*Sometimes*	*Often*	*Always*
a.	I have someone I can turn to for helpful advice about a problem	1	2	3	4	5
b.	I have someone who would help me in times of trouble	1	2	3	4	5
c.	I trust my ability to solve difficult problems	1	2	3	4	5
d.	I am confident about the decisions that I make	1	2	3	4	5
e.	I feel like I'm in control of my own life	1	2	3	4	5
f.	I have ways to help myself when I feel troubled	1	2	3	4	5
g.	I know the abuse was not my fault	1	2	3	4	5
h.	I am able to talk about my thoughts and feelings about the abuse	1	2	3	4	5

PLEASE TURN TO NEXT PAGE

2. How much do you agree with the following statements? Please circle one number from 1 to 5, where 1 is strongly disagree, 5 is strongly agree, and the other numbers represent something in between.

		Strongly disagree				Strongly agree
a.	I was an active participant in setting goals with my counselor(s)	1	2	3	4	5
b.	I have made progress toward my goals	1	2	3	4	5
c.	My counselor(s) helped me develop the skills I needed to be able to meet my goals	1	2	3	4	5
d.	Counseling has given me new ways of looking at abuse	1	2	3	4	5
e.	I have a better understanding about the effects that abuse has had on my life	1	2	3	4	5
f.	I have a better understanding of the choices and resources available to me	1	2	3	4	5
g.	My counselor(s) listened respectfully and took me seriously	1	2	3	4	5
h.	My counselor(s) understood the impact the abuse had on me	1	2	3	4	5
i.	My counselor(s) let me know I am not alone	1	2	3	4	5
j.	My counselor(s) helped me develop a safety plan	1	2	3	4	5
k.	My counselor(s) explained that domestic violence is not only a personal problem but also a social problem	1	2	3	4	5

l. Staff respected my
    racial/ethnic identity...................... 1   2   3   4   5

m. Staff respected my
    cultural customs........................... 1   2   3   4   5

n. Staff respected my
    religious/spiritual
    beliefs and practices 1   2   3   4   5

o. Staff respected my
    sexual orientation 1   2   3   4   5

3. What type of counseling did you receive? *PLEASE CIRCLE ALL THAT APPLY*

Individual counseling... 1

Group counseling 2

Family counseling.. 3

Other (PLEASE SPECIFY)................................. 4

_____

4. About how many counseling sessions did you attend?

1 to 2 sessions 1

3 to 5 sessions 2

6 to 10 sessions 3

11 to 20 sessions 4

More than 20 sessions..................................... 5

5. How long ago did the abuse/assault occur that brought you to this program?

Still occurring... 1

Less than 1 year ago (but it has stopped) 2

1 to 5 years ago.. 3

6 to 10 years ago.. 4

More than 10 years ago 5

6. Sometimes people have had several types of violence in their lives. Are you a survivor of . . .

		Yes	No
a.	Stalking	1	0
b.	Sexual abuse/incest when you were a child?	1	0
c.	Adult sexual assault by a stranger?	1	0
d.	Adult sexual assault by a friend or acquaintance?	1	0
e.	Adult sexual assault by a dating partner?	1	0
f.	Adult sexual assault by husband/wife/partner?	1	0
g.	Sexual harassment?	1	0

7. Other than sexual assault, are you a survivor of physical abuse . . .

		Yes	No
a.	As a child?	1	0
b.	As an adult by a dating partner?	1	0
c.	As an adult by an ex-dating partner?	1	0
d.	As an adult by an intimate partner such as a husband, wife, or significant other?	1	0
e.	As an adult by an ex-intimate partner such as a husband, wife, or significant other?	1	0
f.	As an adult by another family member?	1	0

8. What do you consider your race/ethnicity to be?

African American/Black 1

Hispanic/Latina(o) 2

Asian/Pacific Islander 3

Native American 4

White/Caucasian 5

Other (PLEASE SPECIFY) 6

_____

9. What is your gender?

Female 1

Male 2

10. What is your age?

Less than 18 years old 1

Between 18 and 25 years old 2

Between 26 and 30 years old 3

Between 31 and 35 years old 4

Between 36 and 40 years old 5

Between 41 and 45 years old 6

Between 46 and 65 years old 7

More than 65 years old 8

Thank you again for taking the time to answer these
questions. Your opinion is very important to us so
that we can improve our services.

DOMESTIC VIOLENCE
BRIEF ADVOCACY INTERVIEW

➤ *STAFF SHOULD READ QUESTIONS 1 TO 5 TO SURVIVOR AT END OF ADVOCACY CONTACT*

➤ *ASK ONLY OF VICTIMS AGED 18 OR OLDER—DO NOT USE THIS INTERVIEW FOR CHILDREN OR SIGNIFICANT OTHERS.*

➤ *IF THE VICTIM IS EXTREMELY DISTRESSED AND YOU THINK IT WOULD UPSET HER/HIM FURTHER, DO NOT ASK QUESTIONS 1 TO 5. GO DIRECTLY TO QUESTION 6.*

SECTION A:

1. We are trying to find out how helpful it is to have people from our agency here with you in the (EMERGENCY ROOM/POLICE STATION/COURTROOM). If it's okay with you, I'd like to ask you some questions about how you feel about our time together before we wrap things up. This is voluntary; we do not have to do this if you don't want to. You may stop at any time and nothing you say will affect the services you receive. Your name will never be connected to your answers. Would it be okay if I asked you some questions?

    YES .... 1 ➔ (GO TO Q.2)

    NO .... 0 ➔ (SKIP TO Q.6)

2. I'd like you to feel free to answer honestly so that we can learn more about our services. Because someone from our agency was here with you, how much more information do you have about the choices available to you? Would you say you have . . .

    A lot more information,................................... 4

    Somewhat more information, ... 3

    A little more information, or 2

    No more information? 1

    Did not ask or don't know 99

3. How much support did you get from having someone from our agency here with you? Would you say you felt. . .

    A lot of support, ... 4

    Some support, ... 3

    A little support, or 2

    No support at all? 1

    Did not ask or don't know 99

4. How much did having someone from our agency here help you make decisions about what you want to do? Would you say it helped you . . .

    A lot, ... 4

    Somewhat, ... 3

    A little, or 2

    Not at all? 1

    Did not ask or don't know 99

5. As a result of working with (AGENCY NAME), how much more information do you have about . . .

    a. How the legal process works? Do you have . . .

    Much more information, ... 4

    Somewhat more information, ... 3

    A little more information, or 2

    No more information? 1

    Did not ask or don't know 99

    b. How to get an order of protection? Do you have . . .

    Much more information, ... 4

    Somewhat more information, ... 3

    A little more information, ... 2

    No more information? 1

    Did not ask or don't know 99

c. How to enforce an order of protection? Do you have . . .

Much more information,.. 4

Somewhat more information,.. 3

A little more information, ... 2

No more information? 1

Did not ask or don't know.. 99

d. What the police should do for you? Do you have . . .

Much more information,.. 4

Somewhat more information,.. 3

A little more information, or 2

No more information? 1

Did not ask or don't know.. 99

e. How to get help in a future incident of abuse? Do you have . . .

Much more information,.. 4

Somewhat more information,.. 3

A little more information, or 2

No more information? 1

Did not ask or don't know.. 99

Thank you for answering these questions for me.

➢ *ANSWER THE FOLLOWING QUESTIONS AFTER THE ADVOCACY CONTACT IS OVER*

SECTION B:

6. Were you able to ask questions 1 to 5 of the client? *CIRCLE ONLY ONE CHOICE*

   Yes 1

   No—Survivor did not consent to being
   asked the questions 2

   No—Survivor too upset or distressed or injured 3

   No—Language difficulties 4

   No—Survivor left before could be asked questions 5

   No—Other reason (PLEASE SPECIFY) 6

   _____

7. What type(s) of advocacy did you provide? *CIRCLE ALL THAT APPLY*

   Criminal justice (filing report) 1

   Civil legal advocacy 2

   Medical advocacy 3

   Other advocacy (PLEASE SPECIFY) 4

   _____

8. Where did you provide the services? *CIRCLE ALL THAT APPLY*

   Hospital/medical center 1

   Police station 2

   Courthouse 3

   Domestic violence agency 4

   School 5

   Other (PLEASE SPECIFY) 6

   _____

9. What is the survivor's race/ethnicity? *CIRCLE ALL THAT APPLY*

    African American/Black 1

    Hispanic/Latina(o) 2

    Asian/Pacific Islander 3

    Native American 4

    White/Caucasian 5

    Other (PLEASE SPECIFY) 6

    _____

    Don't know.. 99

10. What is the survivor's gender? *CIRCLE ONLY ONE CHOICE*

    Female 1

    Male 2

11. What is the survivor's approximate age? _____ years old

12. What is the survivor's *primary* language? *CIRCLE ONLY ONE CHOICE*

    English 1

    Spanish 2

    Polish 3

    Russian 4

    Korean 5

    Vietnamese.. 6

    Chinese 7

    Hindi 8

    Urdu 9

    American Sign Language.. 10

    Other (PLEASE SPECIFY) 11

    _____

    Don't know.. 99

13. Did you provide services to significant others, including children?
    CIRCLE ONLY ONE CHOICE

       Yes... 1

       No 0

14. What referrals did you provide to the survivor?

➢ *PLACE AN X OR A ✔ IN THE APPROPRIATE COLUMN.*

  ➢ *Check the first column if you provided a referral within your agency.*

  ➢ *Check the second column if you provided a referral outside your agency.*

  ➢ *Check the third column if you initiated contact with the other service provider for the client (e.g., scheduled an appointment for them).*

  ➢ *Check the fourth column if the service listed was not relevant or not discussed.*

➢ *YOU MAY, OF COURSE, CHECK MORE THAN ONE COLUMN FOR EACH SERVICE LISTED*

		Provided referral within our agency	Provided referral outside agency	Worker initiated contact	Not relevant or not discussed
a.	Additional hotlines				
b.	Attorney referrals				
c.	Called 911 or police				
d.	Community education				
e.	Counseling referrals				
f.	Criminal justice advocacy				
g.	Employment services				
h.	Financial assistance				
i.	Housing services				
j.	Immigration & bilingual services				
k.	Medical advocacy				
l.	Services for children				
m.	Services for offenders				
n.	Shelter				
o.	Substance abuse services				
p.	Testing for HIV/AIDS, STD, pregnancy				
q.	Other (PLEASE SPECIFY)				

DOMESTIC VIOLENCE
EXTENDED ADVOCACY INTERVIEW

➤ *STAFF SHOULD READ QUESTIONS 1 TO 6 ALOUD TO SURVIVOR AT THE END OF THE SESSION*

➤ *ADMINISTER THIS INTERVIEW AFTER THE AVERAGE NUMBER OF ADVOCACY SESSIONS.*

➤ *ASK ONLY OF VICTIMS AGED 18 OR OLDER—DO NOT INTERVIEW CHILDREN OR SIGNIFICANT OTHERS.*

SECTION A:

1. We are trying to find out how helpful our services are, and if it's okay with you, I'd like to ask you some questions about how you feel about our time together before we wrap things up. This is voluntary; we do not have to do this if you don't want to. You may stop at any time, and nothing you say will affect the services you receive. Your name will never be connected to your answers. Would it be okay if I asked you some questions?

   YES ....1➔ (GO TO Q.2)

   NO ....0➔ (SKIP TO Q.7)

2. I'd like you to feel free to answer honestly, so that we can learn more about our services. How much did our program help you with the following?
   For each, please tell me if you felt our program helped very much, somewhat, a little, or not at all.

		Very much	Somewhat	A little	Not at all	Don't know or not relevant
a.	The legal system?	4	3	2	1	99
b.	Housing?	4	3	2	1	99
c.	Employment?	4	3	2	1	99
d.	Education?	4	3	2	1	99
e.	Child care?	4	3	2	1	99
f.	Medical needs?	4	3	2	1	99

g. Material goods like
     food, clothing, or
     supplies? 4   3   2   1   99

h. Money problems? 4   3   2   1   99

i.   Counseling for you, your
     children, or your abuser?..... 4   3   2   1   99

j.   Substance abuse? 4   3   2   1   99

k. Other (PLEASE SPECIFY)... 4   3   2   1   99

_____

3. Because someone from our agency was here with you, how much
    more information do you have about the choices available to you?
    Would you say you have . . .

    A lot more information, ... 4

    Somewhat more information, ... 3

    A little more information, or 2

    No more information? 1

    Did not ask or don't know 99

4. How much support did you get from having someone from our
    agency here with you? Would you say you felt . . .

    A lot of support, ... 4

    Some support, ... 3

    A little support, or 2

    No support at all? 1

    Did not ask or don't know 99

5. How much did having someone from our agency here help you
    make decisions about what you want to do? Would you say it
    helped you . . .

    A lot, ... 4

    Somewhat, ... 3

    A little, or 2

    Not at all? 1

    Did not ask or don't know 99

6. How many times did you meet with someone from our agency?
   CIRCLE ONLY ONE CHOICE

   1 to 3 sessions 1

   4 to 6 sessions 2

   7 to 9 sessions 3

   10 to 12 sessions, or 4

   More than 12 sessions... 5

   Did not ask or don't know... 99

   Thank you for answering these questions.

> ➤ *ANSWER THE FOLLOWING QUESTIONS AFTER THE ADVOCACY CONTACT IS OVER*

SECTION B:

7. What type(s) of advocacy did you provide? *CIRCLE ALL THAT APPLY*

   Criminal justice (filing report) 1

   Civil legal advocacy 2

   Medical advocacy 3

   Other advocacy (PLEASE SPECIFY) 4

   _____

8. Where did you provide the services? *CIRCLE ALL THAT APPLY*

   Hospital/medical center 1

   Police station 2

   Courthouse 3

   Domestic violence agency 4

   School 5

   Other (PLEASE SPECIFY) 6

   _____

9. What is the survivor's race/ethnicity? *CIRCLE ALL THAT APPLY*

   African American/Black 1

   Hispanic/Latina(o) 2

   Asian/Pacific Islander 3

   Native American 4

   White/Caucasian 5

   Other (PLEASE SPECIFY) 6

   _____

   Don't know 99

10. What is the survivor's gender? *CIRCLE ONLY ONE CHOICE*

    Female 1

    Male 2

11. What is the survivor's approximate age?
    _____ years old

12. What is the survivor's *primary* language? *CIRCLE ONLY ONE CHOICE*

    English 1

    Spanish 2

    Polish 3

    Russian 4

    Korean 5

    Vietnamese... 6

    Chinese 7

    Hindi 8

    Urdu 9

    American Sign Language... 10

    Other (PLEASE SPECIFY) 11

    _____

    Don't know.. 99

13. Did you provide services to significant others, including children? *CIRCLE ONLY ONE CHOICE*

    Yes.. 1

    No 0

14.   What referrals did you provide to the survivor?

> *PLACE AN X OR A ✔ IN THE APPROPRIATE COLUMN.*
>> *Check the first column if you provided a referral within your agency.*
>> *Check the second column if you provided a referral outside your agency.*
>> *Check the third column if you initiated contact with the other service provider for the client (e.g., scheduled an appointment for them)*
>> *Check the fourth column if the service listed was not relevant or not discussed.*

> *YOU MAY, OF COURSE, CHECK MORE THAN ONE COLUMN FOR EACH SERVICE LISTED*

		Provided referral within our agency	Provided referral outside agency	Worker initiated contact	Not relevant or not discussed
a.	Additional hotlines				
b.	Attorney referrals				
c.	Called 911 or police				
d.	Community education				
e.	Counseling referrals				
f.	Criminal justice advocacy				
g.	Employment services				
h.	Financial assistance				
i.	Housing services				
j.	Immigration & bilingual services				
k.	Medical advocacy				
l.	Services for children				
m.	Services for offenders				
n.	Shelter				
o.	Substance abuse services				
p.	Testing for HIV/AIDS, STD, pregnancy				
q.	Other (PLEASE SPECIFY)				

INFORMATION SHEET
DOMESTIC VIOLENCE SHELTER
SURVEY

We are asking you to participate in a research project to help us improve our services. We want to know how people feel about living in our shelter, so we are asking everyone who receives shelter to fill out this questionnaire. The questions ask about how comfortable and safe you feel living in this shelter. You may find some of the questions to be upsetting. Your participation is voluntary; you do not have to do this, and you may stop at any time. Your decision whether or not to participate will not affect your relationship with our agency. About 2500 people who receive shelter services from agencies in Illinois will fill out this questionnaire, and your answers will be combined with theirs into one report. Your answers will be kept confidential and your name or other identifying information will not appear in any report. This research may bring no direct benefit to you but it will enable us to improve our services to all our clients.

You have been given an envelope for the questionnaire. If you agree to participate, when you are done with the questionnaire, put it in the envelope, seal the envelope, and put it in the drop box. We will then send it, with those from other people, to be analyzed by qualified researchers at the University of Illinois at Chicago. Your participation or refusal to participate in this research will not affect any relationship that you might have with the University of Illinois at Chicago. No one from this agency will see your individual responses and there is no way that anyone can link your name with your responses. You should not put your name on the questionnaire.

If you have any questions, please ask them now. If you have questions later, you may contact the researcher, Stephanie Riger, at the University of Illinois at Chicago at 312-413-2300. If you have any questions about your rights as a research subject, you may call the Office for Protection of Research Subjects at 312-996-1711. If you decide to participate, please keep this information sheet for your records.

SHELTER EVALUATION SURVEY

Thank you for taking the time to answer these questions. We want to know how helpful our services have been to you and your opinion is important to us. Your answers will be kept confidential. Nothing you say will affect your stay here.

1. How long have you been a resident of this shelter? If you have been here more than once, count this stay only.

   _____ Number of Months

   _____ Number of Weeks

   _____ Number of Days

2. As a resident of this shelter, how safe do you feel here from physical harm by your abuser? Would you say you feel . . .

   Very safe, ... 4

   Somewhat safe, ... 3

   A little safe, or 2

   Not at all safe? 1

3. How safe do you feel here from being contacted by your abuser? Would you say you feel . . .

   Very safe, ... 4

   Somewhat safe, ... 3

   A little safe, or 2

   Not at all safe? 1

4. How comfortable do you feel . . .

	Very comfortable	Somewhat comfortable	A little comfortable	Not at all comfortable
a. Living in the shelter facility?	4	3	2	1
b. Discussing problems at the shelter with shelter staff?	4	3	2	1
c. With the shelter's level of cleanliness?	4	3	2	1

   d. With other residents? 4   3   2   1

   e. Informing staff
       about concerns you
       may have about the living
       conditions within
       the shelter?............................ 4   3   2   1

5. How helpful have other   Very helpful,........................ 4
    residents been to you?   Somewhat helpful, ... 3
                              A little helpful, or 2
                              Not helpful at all? 1

6. How difficult was it to   Very difficult, ... 4
    find out about the shelter?   Somewhat difficult,............. 3
                              A little difficult, or.............. 2
                              Not difficult at all? 1

7. Have other residents
    harmed you,   Yes...................................... 1
    threatened you, or
    stolen from you?   No 0

8. How much do you agree with the following statements?

		Strongly agree	agree	Neither agree nor disagree	disagree	Strongly disagree
a.	Shelter staff respected my racial/ethnic identity 5		4	3	2	1
b.	Shelter staff respected my cultural customs...................... 5		4	3	2	1
c.	Shelter staff respected my religious/cultural beliefs and practices................ 5		4	3	2	1
d.	Shelter staff respected my sexual orientation 5		4	3	2	1

9. What do you consider your
   race/ethnicity to be?

   African American/Black 1
   Hispanic/Latina(o) 2
   Asian/Pacific Islander 3
   Native American 4
   White/Caucasian 5
   Other (PLEASE SPECIFY) .. 6

---

10. What is your gender?

    Female 1
    Male 2

11. What is your age?   _____ years old

Thank you again for taking the time to answer these questions.
Your opinion will help us improve our services.

DOMESTIC VIOLENCE
CRISIS HOTLINE INTERVIEW

➤ *JUST BEFORE HANGING UP, STAFF SHOULD READ THESE QUESTIONS ALOUD AND RECORD THE ANSWERS BELOW.*

➤ *ASK ONLY OF VICTIMS OR SIGNIFICANT OTHERS—DO NOT USE THIS INTERVIEW FOR ANY OTHER CALLERS.*

➤ *IF THE CALLER IS IN CRISIS OR YOU THINK IT WOULD UPSET THE CALLER FURTHER, DO NOT ASK QUESTIONS 1 TO 4. INSTEAD, GO DIRECTLY TO QUESTION 5.*

SECTION A:

1. We are trying to find out how helpful our services are, and if it's okay with you, I'd like to ask you three questions about this phone call before we hang up. This is voluntary; we do not have to do this if you don't want to, or if you've done it before. You may stop at any time, and nothing you say will affect the services you receive. Would it be okay if I asked you the questions?

    Caller consents .... 1 ➔ (GO TO Q.2)

    Caller refuses.......................... 2 ➔ (SKIP TO Q.5)

    Caller has
    previously answered .... 3 ➔ (SKIP TO Q.5)

2. How many times have you called our crisis line before now?

    This is the first time.. 1

    1 to 3 times 2

    4 to 6 times 3

    More than 6 times... 4

    Did not ask or don't know............................... 99

3. I'd like you to feel free to answer honestly, so that we can learn more about our services. As a result of this phone call, how much more information do you have about the choices available to you? Would you say you have . . .

A lot more information, ... 4

Somewhat more information, ... 3

A little more information, or 2

No more information? 1

Did not ask or don't know 99

4. How much support did you get from this phone call? Would you say that this phone call gave you . . .

A lot of support, ... 4

Some support, ... 3

A little support, or 2

No support at all? 1

Did not ask or don't know 99

Thank you for taking the time to answer these questions.

➢ *ANSWER THE FOLLOWING QUESTIONS AFTER COMPLETING THE CALL*

SECTION B:

5. Were you able to ask questions 1 to 4 of the caller? *CIRCLE ONLY ONE CHOICE*

   Yes 1

   No—Caller did not consent to being asked the
   questions 2

   No—Caller had already answered questions before 3

   No—Caller was too upset or distressed 4

   No—Language difficulties 5

   No—Caller hung up 6

   No—Other reason (PLEASE SPECIFY) 7

   _____

6. Who was the caller? *CIRCLE ONLY ONE CHOICE*

   Survivor/victim 1

   Concerned party (e.g., intimate
   partner, friend, parent) 2

   Don't know 99

7. What was the *main* reason for this call? *CIRCLE ONLY ONE CHOICE*

   Emergency-life threatening situation
   (e.g., staff called 911) 1

   Crisis caller is upset, but not in immediate
   danger; staff provided counseling and information 2

   Caller wants shelter 3

   Information and referral 4

   Other reason (PLEASE SPECIFY) 5

   _____

8. Did you discuss things that the caller can do the next time she/he is experiencing similar problems? *CIRCLE ONLY ONE CHOICE*

   Yes 1

   No 0

   Not appropriate/applicable... 99

9. What specific referrals did you provide?

➤ *PLACE AN X OR A ✓ IN THE APPROPRIATE COLUMN.*

   ➤ *Check the first column if you provided a referral within your agency.*
   ➤ *Check the second column if you provided a referral outside your agency.*
   ➤ *Check the third column if you initiated contact with the other service provider for the client (e.g., to schedule an appointment for them).*
   ➤ *Check the fourth column if the service listed was not relevant or not discussed.*

➤ *YOU MAY, OF COURSE, CHECK MORE THAN ONE COLUMN FOR EACH SERVICE LISTED*

		Provided referral within our agency	Provided referral outside agency	Worker initiated contact	Not relevant or not discussed
a.	Additional hotlines				
b.	Attorney referrals				
c.	Called 911 or police				
d.	Community education				
e.	Counseling referrals				
f.	Criminal justice advocacy				
g.	Employment services				
h.	Financial assistance				
i.	Housing services				
j.	Immigration & bilingual services				
k.	Medical advocacy				
l.	Services for children				
m.	Services for offenders				
n.	Shelter				
o.	Substance abuse services				
p.	Testing for HIV/AIDS, STD, pregnancy				
q.	Other (PLEASE SPECIFY)				

Appendix B

Evaluation Measures for Sexual Assault Services

SEXUAL ASSAULT
INFORMATION SHEET
BEFORE COUNSELING SURVEY

We are asking you to participate in a research project to help us improve our services. We want to know how helpful our counseling services are, so we are asking all those who receive counseling to fill out this questionnaire. Some questions ask about past experiences of abuse and about how you are feeling emotionally. You might find some of these questions upsetting. Your participation is voluntary; you do not have to do this and you may stop at any time. Your decision whether or not to participate will not affect your relationship with our agency. About 5,000 people who receive counseling services from agencies in Illinois will fill out this questionnaire and your answers will be combined with theirs into one report. Your answers will be kept confidential and your name or other identifying information will not appear in any report. This research may bring no direct benefit to you but it will enable us to improve our service to all our clients.

You have been given an envelope for the questionnaire. If you agree to participate, when you are done with the questionnaire, put it in the envelope, seal the envelope, and put it in the drop box. We will then send it, with those from other people, to be analyzed by qualified researchers at the University of Illinois at Chicago. No one from this agency will see your individual responses and there is no way that anyone can link your name with your responses. You should not put your name on the questionnaire.

If you have any questions, please ask them now. If you have questions later, you may contact the researcher, Stephanie Riger, at the University of Illinois at Chicago at 312-413-2300. If you have any questions about your rights as a research subject, you may call the Office for Protection of Research Subjects at 312-996-1711. If you decide to participate, keep this information sheet for your records.

_____
Password

BEFORE COUNSELING SURVEY

Thank you for taking the time to answer these questions. We want to know how helpful our counseling services are to you, so your feedback is very important to us. Your answers will be kept confidential. Nothing you say will affect the services that you receive.

PLEASE DO NOT PUT YOUR NAME ON THIS SURVEY

1. How often are the following statements true for you? For each statement in rows "a" through "h," please circle *one* number.

		Never	*Rarely*	*Sometimes*	*Often*	*Always*
a.	I have someone I can turn to for helpful advice about a problem	1	2	3	4	5
b.	I have someone who would help me in times of trouble	1	2	3	4	5
c.	I trust my ability to solve difficult problems	1	2	3	4	5
d.	I am confident about the decisions that I make	1	2	3	4	5
e.	I feel like I'm in control of my own life	1	2	3	4	5
f.	I have ways to help myself when I feel troubled	1	2	3	4	5
g.	I know the sexual assault/ abuse was not my fault	1	2	3	4	5
h.	I am able to talk about my thoughts and feelings about the assault/abuse	1	2	3	4	5

2. Over the past seven days, how often have you been bothered by the following? For each statement in rows "a" through "f," please circle *one* number.

		Never	*Rarely*	*Sometimes*	*Often*	*Always*
a.	Feeling low in energy or slowed down	1	2	3	4	5
b.	Repeated unpleasant thoughts that won't leave your mind	1	2	3	4	5
c.	Sleep that is restless or disturbed	1	2	3	4	5
d.	Feeling bad about yourself	1	2	3	4	5
e.	Feelings of guilt	1	2	3	4	5
f.	Feeling like injuring or hurting yourself	1	2	3	4	5

3. Have you ever called our sexual assault crisis hotline?

    Yes .... 1 → (ANSWER QUESTIONS 4 TO 6)

    No .... 2 → (STOP, TURN IN SURVEY)

    Don't know .... 3 → (STOP, TURN IN SURVEY)

4. How many times have you called our crisis hotline?

    1 to 3 times 1

    4 to 6 times 2

    More than 6 times 3

    Don't know 99

5. After calling the crisis hotline, how much more information did you have about the choices available to you? Would you say you had . . .

    A lot more information, ... 4

    Somewhat more information, ... 3

    A little more information, or 2

    No more information? 1

6. How much support did you get from the crisis hotline? Would you say that the crisis hotline gave you . . .

A lot of support, ... 4

Some support, ... 3

A little support, or 2

No support at all? 1

Thank you again for taking the time to answer these questions. Your opinion is very important to us so that we can improve our services.

SEXUAL ASSAULT
INFORMATION SHEET
COUNSELING SURVEY

We are asking you to participate in a research project to help us improve our services. We want to know how helpful our counseling services are, so we are asking all those who receive counseling to fill out this questionnaire. Some questions ask about past experiences of abuse and about how you are feeling emotionally. You might find some of these questions upsetting. Your participation is voluntary; you do not have to do this and you may stop at any time. Your decision whether or not to participate will not affect your relationship with our agency. About 5,000 people who receive counseling services from agencies in Illinois will fill out this questionnaire and your answers will be combined with theirs into one report. Your answers will be kept confidential and your name or other identifying information will not appear in any report. This research may bring no direct benefit to you but it will enable us to improve our service to all our clients.

You have been given an envelope for the questionnaire. If you agree to participate, when you are done with the questionnaire, put it in the envelope, seal the envelope, and put it in the drop box. We will then send it, with those from other people, to be analyzed by qualified researchers at the University of Illinois at Chicago. No one from this agency will see your individual responses and there is no way that anyone can link your name with your responses. You should not put your name on the questionnaire.

If you have any questions, please ask them now. If you have questions later, you may contact the researcher, Stephanie Riger, at the University of Illinois at Chicago at 312-413-2300. If you have any questions about your rights as a research subject, you may call the Office for Protection of Research Subjects at 312-996-1711. If you decide to participate, keep this information sheet for your records.

COUNSELING SURVEY

Thank you for taking the time to answer these questions. We want to know how helpful our counseling services are to you, so your feedback is very important to us. Your answers will be kept confidential. Nothing you say will affect the services that you receive.

PLEASE DO NOT PUT YOUR NAME ON THIS SURVEY

1. How often are the following statements true for you? For each statement in rows "a" through "h," please circle *one* number.

		Never	Rarely	Sometimes	Often	Always
a.	I have someone I can turn to for helpful advice about a problem	1	2	3	4	5
b.	I have someone who would help me in times of trouble	1	2	3	4	5
c.	I trust my ability to solve difficult problems	1	2	3	4	5
d.	I am confident about the decisions that I make	1	2	3	4	5
e.	I feel like I'm in control of my own life	1	2	3	4	5
f.	I have ways to help myself when I feel troubled	1	2	3	4	5
g.	I know the sexual assault/abuse was not my fault	1	2	3	4	5
h.	I am able to talk about my thoughts and feelings about the assault/abuse	1	2	3	4	5

2. Over the past seven days, how often have you been bothered by the following? For each statement in rows "a" through "f," please circle *one* number.

		Never	*Rarely*	*Sometimes*	*Often*	*Always*
a.	Feeling low in energy or slowed down	1	2	3	4	5
b.	Repeated unpleasant thoughts that won't leave your mind	1	2	3	4	5
c.	Sleep that is restless or disturbed	1	2	3	4	5
d.	Feeling bad about yourself	1	2	3	4	5
e.	Feelings of guilt	1	2	3	4	5
f.	Feeling like injuring or hurting yourself	1	2	3	4	5

3. How much do you agree with each of the following statements? Please circle one number from 1 to 5, where 1 is strongly disagree, 5 is strongly agree, and the other numbers represent something in between.

		Strongly disagree				*Strongly agree*
a.	I was an active participant in setting goals with my counselor(s)	1	2	3	4	5
b.	I have made progress toward my goals	1	2	3	4	5
c.	My counselor(s) helped me develop the skills I needed to be able to meet my goals	1	2	3	4	5
d.	Counseling has given me new ways of looking at sexual assault/abuse	1	2	3	4	5
e.	I have a better understanding about the effects that assault/abuse had on my life	1	2	3	4	5

f. I have a better
    understanding of the
    choices and resources
    available to me 1   2   3   4   5

g. My counselor(s) listened
    respectfully and took
    me seriously........................ 1   2   3   4   5

h. My counselor(s) understood
    the impact the assault
    had on me 1   2   3   4   5

i. My counselor(s) let me
    know I am not alone 1   2   3   4   5

j. My counselor(s) explained
    that sexual assault/abuse
    is not only a personal
    problem, but also a
    social problem 1   2   3   4   5

k. My counselor(s) respected
    my racial/ethnic identity 1   2   3   4   5

l. My counselor(s) respected
    my cultural customs 1   2   3   4   5

m. My counselor(s) respected
    my religious/spiritual beliefs
    and practices 1   2   3   4   5

n. My counselor(s) respected
    my sexual orientation 1   2   3   4   5

4. What type of counseling did you receive? *PLEASE CIRCLE ALL THAT APPLY*

   Individual counseling.. 1

   Group counseling 2

   Both individual and group counseling 3

   Family counseling... 4

   Other (PLEASE SPECIFY).. 5

   _____

5. How many counseling sessions did you attend?

    1 to 2 sessions 1

    3 to 5 sessions 2

    6 to 10 sessions 3

    10 to 20 sessions 4

    More than 20 sessions... 5

6. How long ago did the sexual assault/abuse occur that brought you to this program?

    Still occurring... 1

    Less than 1 year ago (but it has stopped) 2

    1 to 5 years ago... 3

    6 to 10 years ago... 4

    More than 10 years ago 5

7. Sometimes people have had several types of violence in their lives. Are you a survivor of . . .

		Yes	No
a.	Stalking 1		0
b.	Sexual abuse/incest when you were a child? 1		0
c.	Adult sexual assault by a stranger? 1		0
d.	Adult sexual assault by a friend or acquaintance? 1		0
e.	Adult sexual assault by a dating partner?...................... 1		0
f.	Adult sexual assault by husband/wife/partner?............... 1		0
g.	Sexual harassment? 1		0

8. Other than sexual assault, are you a survivor of physical abuse . . .

		Yes	No
a.	As a child?.. 1		0
b.	As an adult by a dating partner? 1		0
c.	As an adult by an ex-dating partner? 1		0
d.	As an adult by an intimate partner such as a husband, wife, or significant other? 1		0

  e. As an adult by an ex-intimate partner
      such as a husband, wife, or significant other? 1   0

  f. As an adult by another family member? 1   0

9. What do you consider your race/ethnicity to be?

      African American/Black 1

      Hispanic/Latina(o) 2

      Asian/Pacific Islander 3

      Native American 4

      White/Caucasian 5

      Other (PLEASE SPECIFY) 6

      _____

10. What is your gender?

      Female 1

      Male 2

11. What is your age?

      Less than 18 years old 1

      Between 18 and 25 years old 2

      Between 26 and 30 years old 3

      Between 31 and 35 years old 4

      Between 36 and 40 years old 5

      Between 41 and 45 years old 6

      Between 46 and 65 years old 7

      More than 65 years old 8

Thank you again for taking the time to answer these questions.
Your opinion is very important to us so that we can improve our
services.

SEXUAL ASSAULT
BRIEF CRIMINAL JUSTICE & MEDICAL ADVOCACY
INTERVIEW

> *STAFF SHOULD READ QUESTIONS 1 TO 4 TO SURVIVOR AT END OF ADVOCACY CONTACT*

> *ASK ONLY OF VICTIMS AGED 18 OR OLDER—DO NOT USE THIS INTERVIEW FOR CHILD SEXUAL ASSAULT CASES. DO NOT INTERVIEW SIGNIFICANT OTHERS.*

> *IF THE VICTIM IS EXTREMELY DISTRESSED AND YOU THINK IT WOULD UPSET HER/HIM FURTHER, DO NOT ASK QUESTIONS 1 TO 4. GO DIRECTLY TO QUESTION 6.*

SECTION A:

1. We are trying to find out how helpful it is to have people from our agency here with you in the (EMERGENCY ROOM/POLICE STATION/COURTS). If it's okay with you, I'd like to ask you some questions about how you feel about our time together before we wrap things up. This is voluntary; we do not have to do this if you don't want to. You may stop at any time and nothing you say will affect the services you receive. Your name will never be connected to your answers. Would it be okay if I asked you some questions?

    YES .... 1➔(GO TO Q.2)

    NO .... 0➔(SKIP TO Q.5)

2. I'd like you to feel free to answer honestly, so that we can learn more about our services. Because someone from our agency was here with you, how much more information do you have about the choices available to you? Would you say you have . . .

    A lot more information, ... 4

    Somewhat more information, ... 3

    A little more information, or 2

    No more information? 1

    Did not ask or don't know 99

3. How much support did you get from having someone from our agency here with you? Would you say you felt . . .

A lot of support, ... 4

Some support, ... 3

A little support, or 2

No support at all? 1

Did not ask or don't know 99

4. How much did having someone from our agency here help you make decisions about what you want to do? Would you say it helped you . . .

A lot, ... 4

Somewhat, ... 3

A little, or 2

Not at all? 1

Did not ask or don't know 99

Thank you for answering these questions.

➢ *ANSWER THE FOLLOWING QUESTIONS AFTER THE ADVOCACY CONTACT IS OVER*

SECTION B:

5. Were you able to ask questions 1 to 4 of the client? *CIRCLE ONLY ONE CHOICE*

   Yes 1

   No—Survivor did not consent to being
   asked the questions 2

   No—Survivor too upset or distressed or injured 3

   No—Language difficulties 4

   No—Survivor left before could be asked questions 5

   No—Other reason (PLEASE SPECIFY) 6

---

6. What type(s) of advocacy did you provide? *CIRCLE ONLY ONE CHOICE*

   Initial criminal justice only (e.g., filing police report) 1

   Initial medical only (e.g., ER exam) 2

   Initial criminal justice and medical 3

7. Where did you provide the services? *CIRCLE ALL THAT APPLY*

   Hospital/medical center 1

   Police station 2

   Courthouse 3

   Sexual assault agency 4

   School 5

   Other (PLEASE SPECIFY) 6

---

8. *FOR CRIMINAL JUSTICE ADVOCACY ONLY—CIRCLE ONLY ONE CHOICE*:
At what point in the process did you start to work with the victim/survivor?

    Before report was filed.. 1

    During filing of report 2

    After report was filed.. 3

    Don't know.. 99

9. *FOR MEDICAL ADVOCACY ONLY—CIRCLE ONLY ONE CHOICE*:
At what point in the process did you start to work with the victim/survivor?

    Before the exam/kit was started 1

    During exam/kit.. 2

    After exam/kit was completed.. 3

    Don't know.. 99

10. What is survivor's race/ethnicity? *CIRCLE ALL THAT APPLY*

    African American/Black 1

    Hispanic/Latina(o) 2

    Asian/Pacific Islander.. 3

    Native American 4

    White/Caucasian 5

    Other (PLEASE SPECIFY) 6

    _____

    Don't know.. 99

11. What is the survivor's gender? *CIRCLE ONLY ONE CHOICE*

    Female 1

    Male 2

12. What is the survivor's approximate age? _____ years old

13. What is the survivor's *primary* language? CIRCLE ONLY ONE
CHOICE

    English 1

    Spanish 2

    Polish 3

    Russian 4

    Korean 5

    Vietnamese 6

    Chinese 7

    Hindi 8

    Urdu 9

    American Sign Language 10

    Other (PLEASE SPECIFY) 11

    _____

    Don't know 99

14. Did you provide services to significant others, family, or friends?
CIRCLE ONLY ONE CHOICE

    Yes.. 1

    No 0

15. What referrals did you provide to the survivor?

➢ *PLACE AN X OR A ✔ IN THE APPROPRIATE COLUMN.*
  ➢ *Check the first column if you provided a referral within your agency.*
  ➢ *Check the second column if you provided a referral outside your agency.*
  ➢ *Check the third column if you initiated contact with the other service provider for the client (e.g., scheduled an appointment for them).*
  ➢ *Check the fourth column if the service listed was not relevant or not discussed.*

➢ *YOU MAY, OF COURSE, CHECK MORE THAN ONE COLUMN FOR EACH SERVICE LISTED*

		Provided referral within our agency	Provided referral outside agency	Worker initiated contact	Not relevant or not discussed
a.	Additional hotlines				
b.	Attorney referrals				
c.	Called 911 or police				
d.	Community education				
e.	Counseling referrals				
f.	Criminal justice advocacy				
g.	Employment services				
h.	Financial assistance				
i.	Housing services				
j.	Immigration & bilingual services				
k.	Medical advocacy				
l.	Services for children				
m.	Services for offenders				
n.	Shelter				
o.	Substance abuse services				
p.	Testing for HIV/AIDS, STD, pregnancy				
q.	Other (PLEASE SPECIFY) _____				

SEXUAL ASSAULT
EXTENDED CRIMINAL JUSTICE AND
MEDICAL ADVOCACY INTERVIEW

> ➤ *STAFF SHOULD READ QUESTIONS 1 TO 4 TO SURVIVOR AT END OF ADVOCACY CONTACT*

> ➤ *ASK ONLY OF VICTIMS AGED 13 OR OLDER—DO NOT USE THIS INTERVIEW FOR CHILD SEXUAL ASSAULT CASES. DO NOT INTERVIEW SIGNIFICANT OTHERS.*

> ➤ *IF THE VICTIM IS EXTREMELY DISTRESSED AND YOU THINK IT WOULD UPSET HER/HIM FURTHER, DO NOT ASK QUESTIONS 1 TO 6. GO DIRECTLY TO QUESTION 7.*

SECTION A:

1. We are trying to find out how helpful our services are, and if it's okay with you, I'd like to ask you some questions about how you feel about our time together before we wrap things up. This is voluntary; we do not have to do this if you don't want to. You may stop at any time and nothing you say will affect the services you receive. Your name will never be connected to your answers. Would it be okay if I asked you some questions?

    YES .... 1➔ (GO TO Q.2)

    NO .... 0➔ (SKIP TO Q.7)

2. I'd like you to feel free to answer honestly, so that we can learn more about our services. How much did our program help you with the following?
    For each, please tell me if you felt our program helped very much, somewhat, a little, or not at all.

		Very much	Some-what	A little	Not at all	Don't know or not relevant
a.	Billing problems related to your hospital visit?	4	3	2	1	99
b.	Follow-up health care?	4	3	2	1	99
c.	Court proceedings?	4	3	2	1	99
d.	Preparing a victim impact statement?	4	3	2	1	99

e. Filing for crime victim's
    compensation?............. 4   3   2   1   99

3. Because someone from our agency was here with you, how much more information do you have about the choices available to you? Would you say you have . . .

A lot more information,.. 4

Somewhat more information, ... 3

A little more information, or 2

No more information? 1

Did not ask or don't know 99

4. How much support did you get from having someone from our agency here with you? Would you say you felt. . .

A lot of support,... 4

Some support,... 3

A little support, or 2

No support at all?... 1

Did not ask or don't know 99

5. How much did having someone from our agency here help you make decisions about what you want to do? Would you say it helped you . . .

A lot,... 4

Somewhat, ... 3

A little, or 2

Not at all?... 1

Did not ask or don't know 99

6. How many times did you meet with someone from our agency? *CIRCLE ONLY ONE CHOICE*

1 to 3 sessions... 1

4 to 6 sessions... 2

7 to 9 sessions 3

10 to 12 sessions, or 4

More than 12 sessions 5

Did not ask or don't know 99

Thank you for answering these questions.

> ➤ *ANSWER THE FOLLOWING QUESTIONS AFTER THE ADVOCACY CONTACT IS OVER*

SECTION B:

7. Were you able to ask questions 1 to 4 of the client? *CIRCLE ONLY ONE CHOICE*

   Yes 1

   No—Survivor did not consent
   to being asked the questions 2

   No—Survivor too upset or distressed or injured 3

   No—Language difficulties 4

   No—Survivor left before could be asked questions 5

   No—Other reason (PLEASE SPECIFY) 6

   _____

8. What type(s) of advocacy did you provide? *CIRCLE ALL THAT APPLY*

   Extended criminal justice (e.g., court case) 1

   Extended medical (e.g., hospital billing problems) 2

   Other (PLEASE SPECIFY) 3

   _____

9. Where did you provide the services? *CIRCLE ALL THAT APPLY*

   Hospital/medical clinic 1

   Police station 2

   Courthouse 3

   Sexual assault agency 4

   School 5

   Other (PLEASE SPECIFY) 6

   _____

10. What is the survivor's race/ethnicity? *CIRCLE ALL THAT APPLY*

    African American/Black 1

    Hispanic/Latina(o) 2

    Asian/Pacific Islander 3

    Native American 4

    White/Caucasian 5

    Other (PLEASE SPECIFY) 6

    _____

    Don't know.. 99

11. What is the survivor's gender? *CIRCLE ONLY ONE CHOICE*

    Female 1

    Male 2

12. What is the survivor's approximate age? _____ years old

13. What is the survivor's *primary* language? *CIRCLE ONLY ONE CHOICE*

    English 1

    Spanish 2

    Polish 3

    Russian 4

    Korean 5

    Vietnamese... 6

    Chinese 7

    Hindi 8

    Urdu 9

    American Sign Language... 10

    Other (PLEASE SPECIFY) 11

    _____

    Don't know.. 99

14. Did you provide services to significant others, family, or friends?
    CIRCLE ONLY ONE CHOICE

    Yes.. 1

    No 0

15. What referrals did you provide to the survivor?

➢ *PLACE AN X OR A ✔ IN THE APPROPRIATE COLUMN.*

  ➢ *Check the first column if you provided a referral within your agency.*
  ➢ *Check the second column if you provided a referral outside your agency.*
  ➢ *Check the third column if you initiated contact with the other service provider for the client (e.g., scheduled an appointment for them).*
  ➢ *Check the fourth column if the service listed was not relevant or not discussed.*

➢ *YOU MAY, OF COURSE, CHECK MORE THAN ONE COLUMN FOR EACH SERVICE LISTED*

		Provided referral within our agency	Provided referral outside agency	Worker initiated contact	Not relevant or not discussed
a.	Additional hotlines				
b.	Attorney referrals				
c.	Called 911 or police				
d.	Community education				
e.	Counseling referrals				
f.	Criminal justice advocacy				
g.	Employment services				
h.	Financial assistance				
i.	Housing services				
j.	Immigration & bilingual services				
k.	Medical advocacy				
l.	Services for children				
m.	Services for offenders				
n.	Shelter				
o.	Substance abuse services				
p.	Testing for HIV/AIDS, STD, pregnancy				
q.	Other (PLEASE SPECIFY)				

SEXUAL ASSAULT
CRISIS HOTLINE INTERVIEW

> ➤ *JUST BEFORE HANGING UP, STAFF SHOULD READ THESE QUESTIONS ALOUD AND RECORD THE ANSWERS BELOW.*

> ➤ *ASK ONLY OF VICTIMS OR SIGNIFICANT OTHERS—DO NOT USE THIS INTERVIEW FOR ANY OTHER CALLERS.*

> ➤ *IF THE CALLER IS IN CRISIS OR YOU THINK IT WOULD UPSET THE CALLER FURTHER, DO NOT ASK QUESTIONS 1 TO 4. INSTEAD, GO DIRECTLY TO QUESTION 5.*

SECTION A:

1. We are trying to find out how helpful our services are, and if it's okay with you, I'd like to ask you three questions about this phone call before we hang up. This is voluntary; we do not have to do this if you don't want to or if you've done it before. You may stop at any time and nothing you say will affect the services you receive. Would it be okay if I asked you the questions?

    Caller consents .... 1➔ (GO TO Q.2)

    Caller refuses .... 2➔ (SKIP TO Q.5)

    Caller has previously
    answered .... 3➔ (SKIP TO Q.5)

2. How many times have you called our crisis line before now?

    This is the first time 1

    1 to 3 times... 2

    4 to 6 times... 3

    More than 6 times 4

    Did not ask or don't know 99

3. I'd like you to feel free to answer honestly so that we can learn more about our services. As a result of this phone call, how much more information do you have about the choices available to you? Would you say you have . . .

> A lot more information,.. 4
>
> Somewhat more information, ... 3
>
> A little more information, or 2
>
> No more information? 1
>
> Did not ask or don't know 99

4. How much support did you get from this phone call? Would you say that this phone call gave you . . .

> A lot of support, ... 4
>
> Some support, ... 3
>
> A little support, or 2
>
> No support at all? 1
>
> Did not ask or don't know 99

Thank you for taking the time to answer these questions.

ANSWER THE FOLLOWING QUESTIONS AFTER COMPLETING THE CALL

SECTION B:

5. Were you able to ask questions 1 to 4 of the caller? *CIRCLE ONLY ONE CHOICE*

      Yes 1

      No—Caller did not consent to being
      asked the questions 2

      No—Caller had already answered questions before 3

      No—Caller was too upset or distressed 4

      No—Language difficulties 5

      No—Caller hung up 6

      No—Other reason (PLEASE SPECIFY) 7

      _____

6. Who was the caller? *CIRCLE ONLY ONE CHOICE*

      Survivor/victim 1

      Concerned party (e.g., intimate
      partner, friend, parent) 2

      Don't know 99

7. What was the *main* reason for this call? *CIRCLE ONLY ONE CHOICE*

      Emergency/life threatening situation

      (e.g., staff called 911) 1

      Crisis caller is upset, but not in immediate danger; staff
      provided counseling and information 2

      Caller wants shelter 3

      Information and referral 4

      Other reason (PLEASE SPECIFY) 5

      _____

8. Did you discuss things that the caller can do the next time she/he is experiencing similar problems? *CIRCLE ONLY ONE CHOICE*

  Yes 1

  No 0

  Not appropriate/applicable 99

9.   What specific referrals did you provide?

➤ *PLACE AN X OR ✔ A IN THE APPROPRIATE COLUMN.*

   ➤ *Check the first column if you provided a referral within your agency.*
   ➤ *Check the second column if you provided a referral outside your agency.*
   ➤ *Check the third column if you initiated contact with the other service provider for the client (e.g., to schedule an appointment for them).*
   ➤ *Check the fourth column if the service listed was not relevant or not discussed.*

➤ *YOU MAY, OF COURSE, CHECK MORE THAN ONE COL-UMN FOR EACH SERVICE LISTED*

		Provided referral within our agency	Provided referral outside agency	Worker initiated contact	Not relevant or not discussed
a.	Additional hotlines				
b.	Attorney referrals				
c.	Called 911 or police				
d.	Community education				
e.	Counseling referrals				
f.	Criminal justice advocacy				
g.	Employment services				
h.	Financial assistance				
i.	Housing services				
j.	Immigration & bilingual services				
k.	Medical advocacy				
l.	Services for children				
m.	Services for offenders				
n.	Shelter				
o.	Substance abuse services				
p.	Testing for HIV/AIDS, STD, pregnancy				
q.	Other (PLEASE SPECIFY) _____				

Additional Resources

1. *Evaluation Handbook for W.K. Kellogg Foundation Grantees: Information on Cluster Evaluation*

   Published by: W.K. Kellogg Foundation
   One Michigan Avenue East
   Battle Creek, MI 49017-4058
   (616) 968-1611
   Available at: www.wkkf.org

2. *Evaluation Guidebook for Projects Funded by S.T.O.P. Formula Grants Under the Violence Against Women Act*

   Published by: Urban Institute
   2100 M Street, N.W.
   Washington, DC 20037
   (202) 833-7200
   paffairs@ui.urban.org
   Publications/UI Press:
   (877) 847-7377 (toll-free)
   pubs@ui.urban.org

3. *Outcome Evaluation Strategies for Domestic Violence Programs: A Practical Guide*

   Author: Sullivan
   Published by: Pennsylvania Coalition Against Domestic Violence
   (800) 537-2238
   (800) 932-4632 (PA only)
   Available at: www.pcadv.org

4. *Outcome Evaluation Strategies for Sexual Assault Service Programs: A Practical Guide*

   Authors: Sullivan & Coats
   Published by: Michigan Coalition Against Domestic and Sexual Violence
   Fax: (517) 347-1377
   Available at: www.mcadsv.org

5. *A Guide to Using Your Evaluation Results*

   Available at: www.uic.edu/depts/psch/idhs

6. *Ethics in Research with Human Participants*

   Authors: Sales & Folkman
   Published by: American Psychological Association
   Available at: www.apa.org

7. *Program Evaluation: Alternative Approaches and Practical Guidelines*

   Authors: Worthen, Sanders, & Fitzpatrick
   Published by: Longman
   Available at: www.longman.awl.com

8. *Evaluating Domestic Violence Programs*

   Authors: Edleson & Frick
   Published by: Domestic Abuse Project
   Available at: www.mincava.umn.edu

9. *Introduction to Evaluation Training and Practice for Sexual Assault Service Delivery*

   Introduction to Evaluation Training and Practice for Sexual Assault Prevention

   Authors: Campbell, Davidson, Ahrens, Aponte, Dorey, Grubstein, Naegeli, & Wasco
   Published by: Michigan Public Health Institute
   2436 Woodlake Circle, Suite 300
   Okemos, MI 48864
   (517) 324-8300
   Fax: (517) 381-0260
   central@mphi.org

10. *Evaluation Handbook for Community Mobilization: Evaluating Domestic Violence Activism*

    Authors: Garske, DeLeon-Granados, Hoffman, Meisel, Rath, & Skinner
    Published by: California Department of Health Services,

Maternal and Child Health Branch, Domestic Violence Section
Available at: www.maws.org

11. *Statements on Ethics: Principles of Professional Responsibility*

Published by: American Anthropological Association
Available at: www.aaanet.org

12. *Guiding Principles for Evaluators*

Published by: American Evaluation Association
Available at: www.eval.org

13. *Ethical Principles of Psychologists and Code of Conduct*

Published by: American Psychological Association
Available at: www.apa.org

References

Abel, E. M. (2000). Psychosocial treatments for battered women: A review of empirical research. *Research on Social Work Practice, 10*(1), 55-77.

Abraham, M. (2000). *Speaking the unspeakable: Marital violence among South Asian immigrants in the United States.* New Brunswick, NJ: Rutgers University Press.

Ahrens, C. E., Campbell, R., Wasco, S. M., Aponte, G., Grubstein, L., & Davidson, W. S. (2000). Sexual assault nurse examiner programs: An alternative approach to medical service delivery for rape victims. *Journal of Interpersonal Violence, 15,* 921-943.

Altman, D. G. (1995). Sustaining interventions in community systems: On the relationship between researchers and communities. *Health Psychology, 14,* 526-536.

Andersen, M. (1981). Corporate wives: Longing for liberation or satisfied with the status quo? *Urban Life, 10,* 311-327.

Berger, R., Searles, P., & Neuman W. (1988). The dimensions of rape reform legislation. *Law and Society Review, 22*(2), 329-357.

Berk, R. A., Newton P. J., & Berk, S. F. (1986). What a difference a day makes: An empirical study of the impact of shelters for battered women. *Journal of Marriage and the Family, 48,* 481-490.

Binder, A., & Meeker, J. W. (1988). Experiments as reforms. *Journal of Criminal Justice, 16,* 347-358.

Block, C. R., Engel, B., Naureckas, S. M., & Riordan, K. A. (1999). Chicago Women's Health Risk Study: Lessons in collaboration. *Violence Against Women, 5,* 1158-1177.

Bordt, R. (1997). *The structure of women's non-profit organizations.* Bloomington: Indiana University Press.

Bourg, S., & Stock, H. V. (1994). A review of domestic violence arrest statistics in a police department using a pro-arrest policy: Are pro-arrest policies enough? *Journal of Family Violence, 9,* 177-189.

Bowman, C. G. (1992). The arrest experiments: A feminist critique. *Journal of Criminal Law and Criminology, 83,* 201-209.

Brown, P. (1995). The role of the evaluator in comprehensive community initiatives. In J. Connell, A. Kubisch, L. Schorr, & C. H. Weiss (Eds.), *New approaches to evaluating community initiatives* (pp. 201-225). Washington, DC: Aspen Institute.

Buzawa, E. S., & Buzawa, C. G. (1990). *Domestic violence: The criminal justice response.* Newbury Park, CA: Sage.

Buzawa, E. S., & Buzawa, C. G. (1993). The scientific evidence is not conclusive: Arrest is no panacea. In R. Gelles & D. Loeske (Eds.), *Current controversies on family violence* (pp. 337-356). Newbury Park, CA: Sage.

Byington, D. B., Martin, P. Y., DiNitto, D. M., & Maxwell, M. S. (1991). Organizational affiliation and effectiveness: The case of rape crisis centers. *Administration in Social Work, 15,* 83-103.

Campbell, J., Dienemann, J., Kub, J., & Wurmser, T. (1999). Collaboration as partnership between a school of nursing and a domestic violence agency. *Violence Against Women, 5,* 1140-1157.

Campbell, R. (1996). *The community response to rape: An ecological conception of victims' experiences.* Unpublished doctoral dissertation, Michigan State University, East Lansing.

Campbell, R. (1998). The community response to rape: Victims' experiences with the legal, medical, and mental health systems. *American Journal of Community Psychology, 26,* 355-379.

Campbell, R., Baker, C. K., & Mazurek, T. (1998). Remaining radical? Organizational predictors of rape crisis centers' social change initiatives. *American Journal of Community Psychology, 26,* 465-491.

Campbell, R., & Bybee, D. (1997). Emergency medical services for rape victims: Detecting the cracks in service delivery. *Women's Health, 3,* 75-101.

Campbell, R., Davidson, W. S., Ahrens, C., Aponte, G., Dorey, H., Grubstein, L., Naegeli, M., & Wasco, S. (1998). *Introduction to evaluation training and practice for sexual assault service delivery.* Okemos, MI: Michigan Public Health Institute.

Campbell, R., Davidson, W. S., Dorey, H., Grubstein, L., & Naegeli, M. (1999). *Evaluation training and practice for sexual assault service delivery, part two (data analysis).* Okemos, MI: Michigan Public Health Institute.

Campbell, R., & Martin, P. Y. (2001). Services for sexual assault survivors: The role of rape crisis centers. In C. M. Renzetti, J. L. Edleson, & R. K. Bergen (Eds.), *Sourcebook on violence against women* (pp. 227-241). Thousand Oaks, CA: Sage.

Campbell, R., Sefl, T., Barnes, H. E., Ahrens, C. E., Wasco, S. M., & Zaragoza-Diesfeld, Y. (1999). Community services for rape survivors: Enhancing psychological well-being or increasing trauma? *Journal of Consulting and Clinical Psychology, 67,* 847-858.

Campbell, R., Sullivan, C. M., & Davidson, W. S. (1995). Women who use domestic violence shelters: Changes in depression over time. *Psychology of Women Quarterly, 19*(2), 237-255.

Cancian, F. M. (1993). Conflicts between activist research and academic success: Participatory research and alternative strategies. *American Sociologist, 24,* 92-106.

Chaudhuri, M., & Daly, K. (1992). Do restraining orders help? Battered women's experience with male violence and the legal process. In E. S. Buzawa & C. G. Buzawa (Eds.), *Domestic violence: The changing criminal justice response* (pp. 227-252). Westport, CT: Auburn House.

Chavis, D., Stucky, P., & Wandersman, A. (1983). Returning basic research to the community: A relationship between scientist and citizen. *American Psychologist, 38,* 424-434.

Chow, E. N. (1989). The feminist movement: Where are all the Asian-American women? In Asian Women United of California (Eds.), *Making waves: An anthology by and about Asian American women* (pp. 362-376). Boston: Beacon.

Collins, B. G., & Whalen, M. B. (1989). The rape crisis movement: Radical or reformist? *Social Work, 34*(1), 61-63.

Crenshaw, K. W. (1994). Mapping the margins: Intersectionality, identity politics and violence against women. In M. A. Fineman & B. Mykitiul (Eds.), *The public nature of private violence* (pp. 93-120). New York: Routledge.

Davis, A. Y. (1985). *Violence against women and the ongoing challenge to racism.* New York: Kitchen Table.

Davis, A. Y. (2000). The color of violence against women. *Colorlines, 3,* 4-8.

DiMaggio, P. J., & Powell, W. W. (1991). Introduction. In W. W. Powell & P. J. DiMaggio (Eds.), *The new institutionalization in organizational analysis* (pp. 1-38). Chicago: University of Chicago Press.

Dobash, R. E., & Dobash, R. (1979). *Violence against wives: A case against patriarchy.* New York: Free Press.

Dobash, R. E., & Dobash, R. P. (1992). *Women, violence, and social change.* London: Routledge.

Dunford, F. (1992). The measurement of recidivism in cases of spousal assault. *Journal of Criminal Law and Criminology, 83,* 122-130.

Dunford, F., Huizinga, D., & Elliot, D. S. (1990). The role of arrest in domestic assault: The Omaha police experiment. *Criminology, 2,* 183-206.

Dutton, D. G., Bodnarchuk, M., Kropp, R., Hart, S. D., & Ogloff, J. R. P. (1997). Wife assault treatment and criminal recidivism: An 11-year follow-up. *International Journal of Offender Therapy and Comparative Criminology, 41*(1), 9-23.

Edleson, J., & Bible, A. L. (2001). Collaborating for women's safety: Partnerships between research and practice. In C. Renzetti, J. L. Edleson, & R. K. Bergen (Eds.), *Sourcebook on violence against women* (pp. 73-95). Thousand Oaks, CA: Sage.

Edleson, J. L., & Frick, C. (1997). *Evaluating domestic violence programs.* Minneapolis: Domestic Abuse Project.

Erez, E. (2000). Immigration, culture conflict and domestic violence/women battering. *Crime Prevention and Community Safety: An International Journal, 2,* 27-36.

Ferraro, K. (1989a). The legal response to women battering in the US. In J. Hamner, J. Radford, & E. A. Stanko (Eds.), *Women, policing, and male violence* (pp. 155-184). London: Routledge & Keegan Paul.

Ferraro, K. (1989b). Policing women battering. *Social Problems, 36,* 61-74.

Fine, M. (1989). The politics of research and activism: Violence against women. *Gender & Society, 3,* 549-558.

Fine, M. (1992). Passions, politics, and power: Feminist research possibilities. In *Disruptive voices: The possibilities of feminist research* (pp. 205-231). Ann Arbor: University of Michigan Press.

Finn, P., & Colson, S. (1990). *Civil protection orders: Legislation, current court practice, and enforcement.* Washington, DC: National Institute of Justice.

Fischer, K., & Rose, M. (1995). When enough is enough: Battered women's decision making around court orders of protection. *Crime and Delinquency, 41,* 414-429.

Frazier, P. A., & Haney, B. (1996). Sexual assault cases in the legal system: Police, prosecutor, and victim perspectives. *Law & Human Behavior, 20,* 607-628.

Frisch, L. (1992). Research that succeeds, policies that fail. *Journal of Criminal Law and Criminology, 83,* 209-216.

Frohmann, L. (1991). Discrediting victims' allegations of sexual assault: Prosecutorial accounts of case rejections. *Social Problems, 38,* 213-226.

Frohmann, L. (1996). "Hard cases": Prosecutorial accounts for filing problematic sexual assault complaints. In H. Lopata & A. F. Figert (Eds.), *Current research on occupations and professions* (Vol. 9, pp. 189-210). Greenwich, CT: JAI.

Garske, D., DeLeon-Granados, W., Hoffman, L., Meisel, J., Rath, C., & Skinner, J. (2000). *Evaluation handbook for community mobilization: Evaluating domestic violence activism.* San Rafael: California Department of Health Services, Maternal and Child Health Branch, Domestic Violence Section.

Gelles, R. J. (1993). Constraints against family violence: How well do they work? In E. S. Buzawa & C. S. Buzawa (Eds.), *Do arrests and restraining orders work?* (pp. 30-43). Newbury Park, CA: Sage.

Gelles, R. J. (1994). Research and advocacy: Can one wear two hats? *Family Process, 33*(1), 93-95.

Gilfus, M., Fineran, S., Jensen, S., Cohan, D., & Hartwick, L. (1999). Researchers and advocates in dialogue. *Violence Against Women, 5,* 1194-1212.

Golding, J. M., Siegel, J. M., Sorenson, S. B., Burnam, M. A., & Stein, J. A. (1989). Social support sources following sexual assault. *Journal of Community Psychology, 17*(1), 92-107.

Gondolf, E., Yllö, K., & Campbell, J. (1997). Collaboration between researchers and advocates. In G. K. Kantor & J. Jasinski (Eds.), *Out of darkness: Contemporary research perspectives on family violence* (pp. 255-267). Thousand Oaks, CA: Sage.

Gordon, M. T., & Riger, S. (1989). *The female fear.* New York: Free Press.

Gorelick, S. (1991). Contradictions of feminist methodology. *Gender & Society, 5,* 459-477.

Gornick, J., Burt, M. R., & Pittman, K. J. (1985). Structure and activities of rape crisis centers in the early 1980s. *Crime & Delinquency, 31,* 247-268.

Hall, B. L. (1992). From margins to center? The development and purpose of participatory research. *American Sociologist, 23*(4), 14-28.

Harre, A., & Smith, B. E. (1996). Effects of restraining orders on domestic violence victims. In E. S. Buzawa & C. S. Buzawa (Eds.), *Do arrests and restraining orders work?* (pp. 214-242). Thousand Oaks, CA: Sage.

Hart, B. (1993). Battered women and the criminal justice system. *American Behavioral Scientist, 36,* 624-638.

Hart, B. (1996). Battered women and the criminal justice system. In E. S. Buzawa & C. S. Buzawa (Eds.), *Do arrests and restraining orders work?* (pp. 98-114). Thousand Oaks, CA: Sage.

Harvey, M. (1985). *Exemplary rape crisis program: Cross-site analysis and case studies.* Washington, DC: National Center for the Prevention and Control of Rape.

Hilton, N. Z. (1994). The failure of arrest to deter wife assault. What now? *Violence Update, 4,* 1-4.

Hirschel, J. D., & Hutchison, I. W. (1992). Female spouse abuse and police response: The Charlotte, North Carolina experiment. *Journal of Criminal Law and Criminology, 83,* 73-119.

Hutchinson, S. A., Wilson, M. P., & Wilson, H. S. (1994). Benefits of participating in research interviews. *Journal of Nursing Scholarship, 26,* 161-164.

Israel, B. A., Schurman, S. J., & Hugentobler, M. K. (1992). Conducting action research: Relationships between organization members and researchers. *Journal of Applied Behavioral Science, 28*(1), 74-101.

Jacobson, N. S. (1994). Rewards and dangers in researching domestic violence. *Family Process, 33*(1), 81-85.

Jang, D., Lee, D., & Frosch, R. M. (1990). Domestic violence in the immigrant and refugee community: Responding to the needs of immigrant women. *Response, 13,* 2-7.

Keiltitz, S., Davis, C., Efkeman, H., Flango, C., & Hannaford, P. (1998). *Civil protection orders: Victim's views on effectiveness.* Washington, DC: U.S. Department of Justice.

Kinports, K., & Fischer, K. (1993). Orders of protection in domestic violence cases: An empirical assessment of the impact of reform statutes. *Texas Journal of Women and the Law, 2,* 163-276.

Klein, A. (1996). Re-abuse in a population of court restrained male batterers: Why retraining orders don't work. In E. S. Buzawa & C. S. Buzawa (Eds.), *Do arrests and restraining orders work?* (pp. 192-213). Thousand Oaks, CA: Sage.

Koss, M. (August, 1998). *Does feminist rape research stand up to attack?* Paper presented at the annual meeting of the American Psychological Association, San Francisco, CA.

Koss, M. P., & Harvey, M. R. (1991). *The rape victim: Clinical and community interventions.* Newbury Park, CA: Sage.

Largen, M. A. (1988). Rape reform law: An analysis. In A. W. Burgess (Ed.), *Sexual assault II.* New York: Garland.

Lather, P. (1986). Research as praxis. *Harvard Educational Review, 56*, 257-277.

Lennett, J., & Colten, M. E. (1999). A winning alliance: Collaboration of advocates and researchers on the Massachusetts Mothers Survey. *Violence Against Women, 5*, 1118-1139.

Levin, R. (1999). Participatory evaluation: Bringing researchers and service providers together as collaborators rather than adversaries. *Violence Against Women, 5*, 1213-1227.

Loh, W. D. (1981). What has rape reform legislation wrought? A truth in criminal labeling. *Journal of Social Issues, 37*(4), 28-52.

Lundy, M., Massat, C. R., Smith, J., & Bhasin, S. (1996). Constructing the research enterprise: Building research bridges between private agencies, public agencies and universities. *Journal of Applied Social Sciences, 20*, 169-176.

Lykes, M. B. (1989). Dialogue with Guatemalan Indian women: Critical perspectives on constructing collaborative research. In R. K. Unger (Ed.), *Representations: Social constructions of gender* (pp. 167-185). Amityville, NY: Baywood.

Madigan, L., & Gamble, N. (1991). *The second rape: Society's continued betrayal of the victim.* New York: Lexington Books.

Marsh, J., Geist, A., & Kaplan, N. (1982). *Rape and the limits of law reform.* Boston: Auburn House.

Martin, D. (1976). *Battered wives.* San Francisco: Glide.

Martin, P. Y. (1997). Gender, accounts, and rape processing work. *Social Problems, 44*, 464-82.

Martin, P. Y., & DiNitto, D. (1987). The rape exam: Beyond the hospital ER. *Women and Health, 12*, 5-28.

Martin, P. Y., DiNitto, D., Byington, D., & Maxwell, M. S. (1992). Organizational and community transformation: The case of a rape crisis center. *Administration in Social Work, 16*(3-4), 123-145.

Martin, P. Y., DiNitto, D., Harrison, D., & Maxwell, S. M. (1985). Controversies surrounding the rape kit exam in the 1980s: Issues and alternatives. *Crime and Delinquency, 31*, 223-246.

Martin, P. Y., & Powell, M. R. (1994). Accounting for the "second assault": Legal organizations' framing of rape victims. *Law and Social Inquiry, 19*, 853-890.

Matoesian, G. M. (1993). *Reproducing rape: Domination through talk in the courtroom.* Chicago: University of Chicago Press.

Matoesian, G. M. (1995). Language, law and society: applied policy implications of the Kennedy rape trial. *Law and Society Review, 29*, 699-702.

Matthews, N. A. (1994). *Confronting rape: The feminist anti-rape movement and the state.* New York: Routledge.

Miller, S. (1989). Unintended side effects of pro-arrest policies and their race and class implications for battered women: A cautionary tale. *Criminal Justice Policy Review, 3*, 299-316.

Miller, S. (1993). Arrest policies for domestic violence and their implications for battered women. In R. Murskin & T. Allens (Eds.), *Women and justice* (pp. 334-359). Englewood Cliffs, NJ: Regents/Prentice Hall.

Moraga, C., & Anzaldua, G. (Eds.). (1981). *This bridge called my back—writings by women of color.* Watertown, MA: Persephone Press.

Moran-Ellis, J. (1996). Close to home: The experience of researching child sexual abuse. In M. Hester, L. Kelly, & J. Radford (Eds.), *Women, violence and male power* (pp. 176-187). Buckingham, UK: Open University Press.

Narayan, U. (1995). Male-order brides: Immigrant women, domestic violence and immigration law. *Hypatia, 10*, 104-119.

National Victim Center. (1992). *Rape in America.* Arlington, VA: Author.

Nyden, P., & Wiewel, W. (1992). Collaborative research: Harnessing the tensions between researcher and practitioner. *American Sociologist, 23*(4), 43-55.

O'Sullivan, E. A. (1978). What has happened to rape crisis centers? A look at their structure, members, and funding. *Victimology, 3,* 45-62.

Pagelow, M. D. (1981). *Woman battering: Victims and their experiences.* Beverly Hills, CA: Sage.

Park, P. (1992). The discovery of participatory research as a new scientific paradigm: Personal and intellectual accounts. *American Sociologist, 23*(4), 29-42.

Petras, E. M., & Porpora, D. V. (1993). Participatory research: Three models and an analysis. *American Sociologist, 24*(1), 107-126.

Pizzey, E. (1974). *Scream quietly or the neighbours will hear.* London: Enslow.

Polk, K. (1985). Rape reform and criminal justice processing. *Crime and Delinquency, 31,* 191-205.

Pride, A. (1981). To respectability and back: A ten year view of the anti-rape movement. In F. Delacoste & F. Newman (Eds.), *Fight back: Feminist resistance to male violence* (pp. 114-118). Minnesota: Cleis Press.

Rasche, C. (1988). Minority women and domestic violence: The unique dilemmas of battered women of color. *Journal of Contemporary Criminal Justice, 4,* 150-171.

Reason, P. (1993). Sitting between appreciation and disappointment: A critique of the Special Edition of *Human Relations* on action research. *Human Relations, 46,* 1253-1270.

Renzetti, C. (1997). Confessions of a reformed positivist: Feminist participatory research as good social science. In M. D. Schwartz (Ed.), *Researching sexual violence against women: Methodological and personal perspectives* (pp. 131-143). Thousand Oaks, CA: Sage.

Richie, B. (2000). A black feminist reflection on the anti-violence movement. *Signs: Journal of Women and Culture in Society, 25,* 1133-1137.

Riger, S. (1984). Vehicles for empowerment: The case of feminist movement organizations. *Prevention in Human Services, 3*(2-3), 99-117.

Riger, S. (1992). Epistemological debates, feminist voices: Science, social values, and the study of women. *American Psychologist, 47,* 730-740.

Riger, S. (1994). Challenges of success: Stages of growth in feminist organizations. *Feminist Studies, 20,* 275-300.

Riger, S. (1999). Working together: Challenges in collaborative research on violence against women. *Violence Against Women, 5,* 1099-1117

Saegert, S. (1993). Charged contexts: Difference, emotion and power in environmental design research. *Architecture & Comportment, 9,* 69-84.

Schechter, S. (1982). *Women and male violence.* Boston: South End Press.

Schewe, P. A., & O'Donohue, W. T. (1993). Sexual abuse prevention with high-risk males: The roles of victim empathy and rape myths. *Violence and Victims, 8,* 336-348.

Schmidt, J. D., & Sherman, L. W. (1993). Does arrest deter domestic violence? The impact of arrest on domestic assault [Special issue]. *American Behavioral Scientist, 36,* 601-609.

Sherman, L. W. (1992). *Policing domestic violence: Experiments and dilemmas.* New York: Free Press.

Sherman, L. W., & Berk, R. A. (1984). The specific deterrent effects of arrest for domestic assault. *American Sociological Review, 49,* 261-272.

Sherman, L. W., Schmidt, J., & Rogan, D. (1992). *Policing domestic violence: Experiments and dilemmas.* New York: Free Press.

Smith, A. (2001, Winter). The color of violence. *Colorlines,* 14-15.

Spalter-Roth, R., & Schreiber, R. (1995). Outsider issues and insider tactics: Strategic tensions in the women's policy network during the 1980s. In M. M. Ferree & P. Y. Martin (Eds.), *Feminist organizations: Harvest of the new women's movement* (pp. 105-127). Philadelphia: Temple University Press.

Spohn, C., & Horney, J. (1992). *Rape law reform: The grassroots revolution and its impact.* New York: Plenum.

Stanko, E. (1997). "I second that emotion": Reflections on feminism, emotionality, and research on sexual violence. In M. D. Schwartz (Ed.), *Researching sexual violence against women: Methodological and personal perspectives* (pp. 74-85). Thousand Oaks, CA: Sage.

Stanko, E. A. (1989). Missing the mark? Police battering. In J. Hamner, J. Radford, & E. A. Stanko (Eds.), *Women, policing, and male violence* (pp. 46-49). London: Routledge & Keegan Paul.

Sullivan, C. M. (1998). *Outcome evaluation strategies for domestic violence programs: A practical guide.* Harrisburg: Pennsylvania Coalition Against Domestic Violence.

Sullivan, C. M., & Bybee, D. I. (1999). Reducing violence using community-based advocacy for women with abusive partners. *Journal of Consulting and Clinical Psychology, 67*(1), 43-53.

Sullivan, C. M., Tan, C., Basta, J., Rumptz, M., & Davidson, W. S. (1992). An advocacy intervention project for women with abusive partners: Initial evaluation. *American Journal of Community Psychology, 20,* 309-332.

Ullman, S. (1996). Do social reactions to sexual assault victims vary by support provider? *Violence and Victims, 11,* 143-156.

Weisz, A. N. (1999). Legal advocacy for domestic violence survivors: The power of an informed relationship. *Families in Society, 80,* 138-147.

Weisz, A. N., Tolman, R. M., & Bennett, L. W. (1998). An ecological study of non-residential services for battered women within a comprehensive community protocol for domestic violence. *Journal of Family Violence, 13,* 395-415.

Wiewel, W., & Lieber, M. (1998). Goal achievement, relationship building, and incrementalism: The challenges of university-community partnerships. *Journal of Planning Education and Research, 17,* 291-301.

Williams, J. E. (1984). Secondary victimization: Confronting public attitudes about rape. *Victimology, 9*(1), 66-81.

Worthen, B. R., Sanders, J. R., & Fitzpatrick, J. L. (1997). *Program evaluation: Alternative approaches and practical guidelines* (2nd ed.). White Plains, NY: Longman.

Zorza, J. (1992). The criminal law of misdemeanor violence, 1970-1990. *Journal of Criminal Law and Criminology, 83,* 46-72.

Author Index

Subject Index

About the Authors

Stephanie Riger is Professor of Psychology and Gender and Women's Studies at the University of Illinois at Chicago. She is the recipient of the American Psychological Association's Division 27 award for Distinguished Contributions to Research and Theory and a two-time winner of the Association for Women in Psychology's Distinguished Publication Award. She is author of *Transforming Psychology: Gender in Theory and Practice* (2000) as well as numerous journal articles and other books. Her current research focuses on the impact of welfare reform on intimate violence and the evaluation of domestic violence and sexual assault services.

Larry Bennett is Associate Professor, Jane Addams College of Social Work, University of Illinois at Chicago. His research interests include the implementation of evidence-based practice in social service agencies, the relationship between substance abuse and domestic violence, the structure and effectiveness of community-based batterers intervention programs, and the links between various forms of men's violence such as bullying, sexual harassment, dating violence, and adult partner abuse. He was a member of the Consensus Panel on Family Violence of the U.S. Center for Substance Abuse Treatment and currently chairs the Illinois Substance Abuse and Domestic Violence Interdisciplinary Task Force. He is a licensed clinical social worker in the State of Illinois, limiting his practice to court-ordered child custody evaluation.

Sharon M. Wasco is a research assistant, instructor, and doctoral candidate in the Department of Psychology at the University of Illinois at Chicago. She is a student affiliate of the American Evaluation

Association and the Society for Community Research and Action (Division 27 of the American Psychological Association). In recent years, she has assisted in developing evaluation materials for sexual assault and domestic violence programs and has provided training and program-specific technical assistance to service providers implementing evaluations in both Michigan and Illinois. She is interested in the effects of gender-based violence on victims, their support networks, and communities. She works with her faculty advisor, Dr. Rebecca Campbell, researching how service providers, organizations, and systems respond to sexual violence against women.

Paul A. Schewe is a prevention researcher at the University of Illinois at Chicago. He is a clinical/community psychologist with extensive experience in developing and evaluating school-based violence prevention programs. In recent years, he has worked on a variety of projects ranging from evaluations of single programs to community-based collaborations to statewide initiatives. The focus of these efforts has included sexual assault, teen dating violence, and domestic violence prevention programs as well as early childhood interventions to promote social-emotional development. He is the editor of *Preventing Relationship Violence Across the Lifespan* (2002) and author of numerous articles on sexual assault prevention and related topics. He is a home-schooling father of three children and contributes to his local community as a scout leader and soccer coach.

Lisa Frohmann is Associate Professor in the Department of Criminal Justice at the University of Illinois at Chicago. For 20 years she has been working in the area of violence against women as both a researcher and an activist. Her research focuses on the prosecution of domestic violence and sexual assault cases and the social construction of race, class, and gender in the law. She is also working on new research, The Autobiographical Photography Project, that examines battered women's conceptions of "safety" as expressed through photography and narrative. Her activist work includes serving as a rape crisis hotline advocate and as an instructor in women's self-defense techniques. She has consulted with sexual assault and domestic violence agencies to provide in-service training on case prosecution and women's experience in court, develop evaluation tools, and navigate organizational change. She also serves on the Board of Directors' Evaluation Committee of Heartland Alliance, which ensures that all research conducted in affiliated organizations meets strict ethical standards.

Jennifer M. Camacho is an epidemiologist with the Chicago Department of Public Health, where she works as internal evaluator.

She received her master's degree from the University of Illinois at Chicago in Community Prevention and Research, where she studied violence against women, program evaluation, and statistics. She regularly teaches informal courses on the use of nonparametric statistics in the evaluation of small programs and enjoys doing independent evaluative and statistical consulting. In addition to violence against women, her research interests include organizational responses to persons with disabilities. Publications for this year include work on community interventions for persons with disabilities and work on the radiating impact of domestic violence.

Rebecca Campbell is Associate Professor of Community/ Quantitative Psychology at the University of Illinois at Chicago. Her current research includes studies on the community response to rape, vicarious trauma among violence against women researchers and service providers, and the evaluation of rape crisis center services. She is the author of *Emotionally Involved: The Impact of Researching Rape* (2001). She received the 2000 Louise Kidder Early Career Award from the Society for the Psychological Study of Social Issues (Division 9) of the American Psychological Association. To get a break from thinking about violence against women, she enjoys gardening and cooking.